D0095768

WRITING AT WORK

HF
5718
J23
1985

WRITING AT WORK

DOs, DON'Ts, and HOW TOs

by ERNST JACOBI

Ten Speed Press

For Lenore, again

Copyright © 1985 by Ernst Jacobi. All rights reserved. No part of this book may be reproduced in any form, except for brief reviews, without the written permission of the publisher.

🔟

Ten Speed Press
P.O. Box 7123
Berkeley, CA 94707

Cover Design by Brenton Beck
Book Design by Hal Hershey
Typography by Skillful Means Press, Oakland, California

Library of Congress Cataloging in Publication Data

Jacobi, Ernst
  Writing at work: DO's, DON'Ts, and HOW TOs

  Includes index.
  1. Communication in management.   2. English
language—Rhetoric.   I. Title.
HF5718.J23   658.4'53   76-13607

Previous edition published by Hayden Book Company in 1976
ISBN 0-8104-5730-X
ISBN 0-8104-5729-6 pbk.

New, updated and expanded edition published by Ten Speed Press.
ISBN 0-89815-147-3

Printed in the United States of America

10   9   8   7   6   5   4   3   2   89   88   87   86

Contents

Part Three.   HOW TOs

Appendices

Introduction

This is not a book on grammar, syntax, and the correct use of words. I am addressing myself to men and women who are in college, business, or the professions and can, therefore, be expected to possess an adequate vocabulary and be able to write an adequate grammatical sentence. What cannot necessarily be expected is that their writing also will be effective. The major change I hope to accomplish through this book is to turn writers into communicators.

Communicating is like making love. If your partner—the person you're communicating with—is bored, the communication isn't going to be enjoyable or successful. There has to be a responsive spark, some degree of reciprocated interest before you can implant whatever message you wish to communicate. Communication is intercourse. This simple truth is all too often lost sight of by people who teach and write about the art of communication. Traditionally the emphasis is on clarity: "Write it clearly and your communication problems are solved. Prefer short words to long ones, simple words to those that smack of academe and erudition. Keep your sentences short and your 'fog count' low, and all your difficulties in making yourself understood will dissolve and disappear."

Without necessarily disputing or denying the merits of these precepts, I submit that clarity isn't enough. I've seen some of the dullest drivel written in clear and lucid prose. Some of mankind's most influential thought has been presented in turgid and difficult form.

Form without substance is meaningless. Substance without form creates needless difficulties. But if there must be a choice, there is no question that in the long run the world will choose substance over form, interest over mere clarity. For whatever else you may have to offer as added inducements, to be effective your communication has to be interesting—first and last. This is the major point I make in this book.

Then how is this book different from other books on writing? First, it is written for the person with no particular interest in becoming a professional writer—the occasional writer for whom writing is not an end in itself but who needs to write in order to function in his occupation and further his career. The person who can benefit from this book can be an executive or a professional, a student or a teacher, an administrator or a secretary. He or she may be an engineer or a scientist, a salesman, doctor, lawyer, fund raiser, house-organ editor, or accountant. All of them will at one time or another need to write a report, a memorandum, or a letter. Almost everybody in almost every occupation has a frequent need to communicate information and ideas.

The principles governing this kind of writing are the same regardless of one's field—and this is a second difference: I stress principles, not mechanical rules. Writing is an art, even in the humble context we are talking about, and any form of art tends to resist rules. Rules seem to make things easier. You can learn them, apply them, and never again make a decision about them. The trouble is, I haven't found any rules that apply all the time, and very few that apply most of the time. Decision-making is an unavoidable part of writing.

Writing is difficult. Let no one tell you that it isn't. It is difficult because it requires an assortment of activities generally classified as thinking, one of the most exhausting—and satisfying—occupations known to man. Thinking encompasses such diverse activities as organizing, musing, formulating, analyzing, anticipating, and penetrating. All these, at one time or another, become involved in the writing process. Writing is difficult because you are trying to communicate without benefit of the feedback that, in conversation, allows you to stagger toward clarity and comprehension, wander around a subject to come to grips with it, and backtrack if a listener's response shows puzzlement. In writing you have to communicate with your readers by first organizing your thoughts, anticipating objections, removing fuzziness, and, most important, analyzing and penetrating your subject. You must discover what you really want to say—something that cannot be taken for granted. This close connection between writing and thinking is stressed throughout this book. You cannot write well unless you thoroughly understand what you are writing about. Insight and understanding are basic requirements. They allow for no short-cuts.

Most authors and teachers of writing stress words, sentences, and paragraphs as the elements of style. I stress something I call the "communicative attitude." It distinguishes the professional writer, whose livelihood depends on being read, from the occasional writer, who frequently takes his reader for granted. It is the communicative attitude that determines a writer's approach, his choice of words—his style. Ultimately this attitude is the principal determinant of a writer's effectiveness.

Carrying out this general approach, I have divided this book into three parts. The DOs of the first part emphasize the principles of effective writing, including specific recommendations on what you can do to make your writing lively, forceful, and interesting. The DON'Ts of the second part deal with common mistakes made by inexperienced writers and sometimes even by skilled ones who have let themselves slip into sloppy habits. The HOW TOs of the third part are a concise guide to handling practical problems.

Part One

DOs

1 ✍️ Write It as You'd Write a Letter to a Friend

Legend has it that novelist Thomas Wolfe emerged from his Greenwich Village apartment one morning and started down the street shouting to passersby: "I wrote thirty pages last night! I wrote thirty pages last night!"

Whether or not the story is true, it strikes a responsive chord in all writers. Many among us freeze at the prospect of merely writing a simple letter. We all dream of producing thirty pages of manuscript in one sitting and are jubilant when we do. To write without sweat and tears is the one wish all writers have in common. We wish for greater fluency and release from the heavy labor of setting words down on a blank sheet of paper. How to do this is a persistent concern of those who wish to improve their writing.

There may be some writers in this world who never get stuck, writers whose fluency is so great that it carries them without a break from the beginning to a predetermined end. I am not one of them. I get stuck with depressing regularity, and I find that the best way to become unstuck is to start over as if I were writing a letter to a friend. This prescription also seems to work well for others who have tried it.

Writing in the form of a letter to a friend gives you several immediate advantages. It forces you to focus on one specific person, preferably one whom you respect and especially like; this immediately influences your communicative attitude. You will tend to be warm, direct, informal, and spontaneous. You will instinctively take care to stress why you are writing and why you think that what you are writing will be of interest. And you will probably avoid being pompous, stiff, and self-important. You are, after all, writing to a friend. You are not trying to impress him. You know he knows you're not stupid, and you need not be afraid of his (or her) criticism. At least that's the kind of friend you should write the letter to—someone at your own level whose weaknesses and failings you know as well as he knows yours.

For the sake of authenticity, you might as well write the salutation and the introductory words meant only for your friend. It puts you in the right mood and costs you very little. Later, when you look over what you have written, you can eliminate these few opening lines and the body of your piece will probably remain structurally sound. But the irrelevant lines usually have to be written to put you in the proper frame of mind.

One great advantage of using this technique is that it helps you clarify what you *really* want to say. Very often, not knowing this can be a major stumbling block. Sometimes we concentrate so hard on our subject that we tend to lose sight of our purpose.

By considering the subject from various angles and by debating with yourself, you build a dynamic tension that can carry you through to the end. In the process of this questioning and debating you might even discover something about the subject itself that you weren't aware of before you started.

Another advantage of the technique is that it tends to free you from self-consciousness. Self-consciousness is probably the greatest single obstacle to good communication. It makes your writing stiff and lifeless. Moreover, when you start weighing every word, you cripple yourself as a writer. This is something that happens to great writers as well as hacks; it is one aspect of the "writing block." Some writers break it by taking a walk, or getting drunk. Some never break it, and give up writing altogether. Deadlines, especially if writers are hungry enough to respect them, will help most of them over the block. But what if you don't have an assignment deadline? Writing your piece like a letter can help in this case. It frees you from the necessity of weighing your words and allows you the luxury of being sloppy. You can always polish the second time around. The important thing is to get something down on paper.

If you have no problem with fluency, the letter format can still be helpful in making you a better communicator. It will help you be more direct and to the point. One of my students once brought me a twenty-page paper on Zen Buddhism. He had a great deal of information but lacked a point of view and a theme. I suggested that he rewrite the piece in the form of a letter to a friend. Perversely, he now began losing his fluency and having difficulties. Difficulties can be a good thing, of course. I would suspect the writer who never experiences them. This Zen philosopher's difficulty in writing to a friend was that it was now no longer enough to explain Zen Buddhism; he also had to tell the friend why he was explaining it. By focusing on a specific person, he forced himself to assume a different posture. He could no longer let his exposition merely lie there passively, as it had before. He had to argue and debate, to propose and defend. From something that had been dull and boring, he developed a piece that was lively and interesting. And he did it all by changing his format. At least this was the conscious change he made. What he actually did was change his stance. He assumed the communicative attitude.

The letter format can also be used for warming up. Unless you are one of those rare people who can write a first draft that needs no revision, you won't lose a thing by writing a few paragraphs in the beginning that may have to be thrown away at the end. What you gain by this warm-up exercise is the necessary momentum for writing with pace and rhythm. If you try to write printable copy from a cold start, you may at times succeed, but you will frustrate yourself more often than not.

Writing a letter to a friend is not a panacea, but it goes a long way toward solving a lot of writing problems. It helps you to loosen up and get the cobwebs out of your brain. I try it whenever I find myself in a bind, and it frequently straightens me out.

Examples

Dear Bob: I'm commissioned to do a piece on the Levelers and am having trouble getting started. As you may or may not know, the Levelers were a group of political agitators who were active before, and for a short time after, the first English Revolution. They were long overlooked and forgotten by history, mainly, I suppose, because they were quite ineffective, almost Quixotic, in what they tried to accomplish, which was to bring a measure of democracy to England a century and a half before the French and American revolutions. Although numerically they represented a majority of the people, they allowed themselves to be totally checked and intimidated by Cromwell and his followers, who overawed them with their self-confidence and moral authority.

I think that's the trouble with the English to this day. Has it ever occurred to you that when you walk down a London street you can tell at a glance, without listening to the accent or looking at how a person is dressed, whether he or she belongs to the lower, middle, or upper class? You can't do this in New York or Paris, and I think the reason is precisely the one I mentioned, that the English lost their democratic revolution, whereas the French and we Americans won ours—or at least labor under the collective illusion that we did.

At this point I realized that I'd found my angle and could proceed without much difficulty.

Dear Irene: I have just spoken to a beautiful lady, Jill Kinmont, the girl who was on her way to becoming an Olympic skiing champion twenty years ago when she shattered her spine just below the neck and became a quadriplegic. She's a teacher now and somehow manages to make you forget that she is severely disabled. She's amazing. She's still a champion.

I stopped my letter. I had found my beginning—What makes a champion a champion?

Here is an example from my work as a technical editor. On the left is the actual input; on the right is the letter I wrote in an effort to clarify the input to myself.

If the XPSD instruction is executed in an interrupt or trap location as the result of an interrupt or a trap, bit 10 of XPSD determines how the indirect reference address (if XPSD is indirectly addressed) and the effective address of XPSD are to be interpreted in addressing memory. If bit 10 of XPSD is a 1, the indirect reference address and the effective address are both treated as virtual addresses, in which case both addresses are transformed through the memory map if the computer is currently in the mapping mode (i.e., if bit 9 of PSD, the current program status doubleword, is also a 1). The indirect reference address and the effective address are used as actual addresses if the computer is currently in the nonmapping mode (i.e., if bit 9 of the current program status doubleword is a 0). However, if bit 10 of XPSD is a 0, the indirect reference address and the effective address are both used as actual addresses regardless of whether the computer is currently in the mapping mode or in the nonmapping mode.

The operation of an XPSD instruction that is not executed in an interrupt or trap location as the result of an interrupt or trap is the same as the above case in that bit position 10 of XPSD does not affect how the indirect reference address is to be interpreted in addressing memory. If XPSD is indirectly addressed, the indirect reference address is transformed through the memory map if the computer is currently in the mapping mode or

Dear Wife: Help! I've been reading this over and over and can't make head or tail of it. Let me try to explain it to you to possibly make it clear to myself. You don't have to understand anything about computers or know the computer terminology used here. Just consider XPSD and PSD as names and don't worry about their meaning.

First we must deal with bit 10 of XPSD. If the bit is on (equals 1), then both types of addresses are treated as virtual addresses; if it is off (equals 0), both are treated as actual addresses. But then there are two conditions attached to this: (1) that the instruction is executed in an interrupt or trap location, and (2) that the computer is currently in the mapping mode (bit 9 of PSD equals 1). In other words, the two bits work in conjunction with each other, and we seem to have two different paths to follow depending on whether or not the instruction is executed in an interrupt or trap location as the result of an interrupt or trap. (This is not redundant and must be stated in this form.) So now I can make myself a truth table and try to rewrite this mess. (See Table 1-1.)

Bit 10 of XPSD together with bit 9 of PSD controls the use of the memory map in interpreting the instruction address. The unshaded area of the truth table below shows the control logic for an XPSD instruction executed in an interrupt or trap location as a result of an interrupt or trap. If the instruction is not the result of an interrupt or the indirect address is used as an actual address if the computer is currently in the nonmapping mode. As in the above case, the effective address is transformed through the memory map if bit 10 of XPSD is a 1 and the computer is currently in the mapping mode. The effective address is used as an actual address if bit 10 of XPSD is a 0 or if the computer is currently in the nonmapping mode.

a trap (shaded area of table), the logic is the same with one exception: Mapping is used in interpreting an indirect reference address even if bit 10 of XPSD equals 0, provided bit 9 of PSD equals 1.

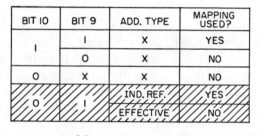

BIT 10	BIT 9	ADD. TYPE	MAPPING USED?
I	I	X	YES
	O	X	NO
O	X	X	NO
O	I	IND. REF.	YES
		EFFECTIVE	NO

Table 1–1. Truth Table

2 Be Interesting

Clarity Isn't Enough

Most people who want to improve their writing think in terms of learning to write clearly. Unquestionably this is essential—but it isn't enough. If you want people to read what you write, you must also know how to interest them.

Your tacit assumption is that what you have to say will be of interest to your readers. You don't write just for yourself. You write to communicate—to touch another's mind or heart. You write because you want to be read.

Unfortunately, in today's world the competition for attention is so intense and the aversion to the printed word so strong that you won't be read, or won't be read properly, unless you can arrange to enlist the cooperation of your readers. And you can do this only by arousing and maintaining their interest.

No book, no person can teach you how to be interesting; but you can learn how to present things that are of interest to you so that they'll be of interest to your reader, too. This is fairly simple when your reader is one specific person, but the task becomes progressively harder as your audience becomes larger and less specific. However, the principles of what makes something interesting remain the same, whether you write for one reader or ten million readers. These principles are discussed in the following chapters and can be summarized as the Eleven Jacobi Commandments:

1. BE RELEVANT. Make it clear from the first word that what you are writing is of importance to your intended reader, and give him reasons why it is important. Your message may help him solve a problem, save him money, improve his performance, or simply make him aware of something that he should know. Relevance means that the writer's message has some importance for the reader. And the careful writer will establish this importance, not by saying "this is important!" but by going directly to the heart of the problem.

2. BE RESPONSIVE. Being responsive is closely related to being relevant but applies generally only to writing that has been solicited (such as reports and proposals), where relevance can be taken for granted. Nothing kills interest more efficiently than failure to be responsive. Imagine your irritation if you need information on oranges and get a report on apples.

3. HAVE SOMETHING TO SAY. Obviously you cannot hope to interest anybody unless there is some substance to your message. Since every writer is a unique individual writing in a unique context, finding something to say is not all that difficult. No writer is skillful enough to get by on words alone. Too many, unfortunately, try. It never works.

4. HAVE A POINT OF VIEW. Having a point of view means recognizing yourself as the filter through which all data must pass on their way to the outside world. Although it is impossible not to have a point of view, an astonishing number of inexperienced writers will try to hide it, thinking it detracts from their objectivity. It does not. A point of view does create distortion, but the kind of distortion that is necessary for communication. Like proper lighting, a point of view selectively emphasizes things that are important while deemphasizing those that are not.

5. USE PERSPECTIVE. Perspective is the necessary corollary to point of view. Where point of view distorts, perspective compensates for the distortion by putting distance between the viewer and the object

viewed. Perspective lets you recognize that the trees constitute the forest.

6. FIND A THEME. The theme needn't be stated directly, but it is the glue that holds your sentences and paragraphs together. Theme is the unifying element, the catalyst that makes words coalesce into a whole.

7. SELECT YOUR POINT OF ATTACK. Whether you write a report, an essay, a user's manual, or a sales letter, you must raise your subject somewhere. The point where you decide to start is your point of attack—a term borrowed from the vocabulary of the dramatist who can't afford to waste time leading his audience into the heart of his story. You can't waste time either, if you want to keep your reader's attention.

8. BE SPECIFIC. For most readers, abstractions and generalizations are foolproof means of inducing sleep. Specific events, specific cases, specific examples are the elements that sustain your reader's interest.

9. GIVE REASONS. Most readers are more interested in why something happens in a certain way than they are in the event itself. Don't be afraid of being pedantic or overtechnical in giving reasons. You'll have to use some judgment, of course, but in most cases your reader will be grateful for the explanation.

10. WRESTLE WITH YOURSELF. You probably did not find your point of view or reach your conclusions without some kind of struggle. Stating the considerations and counterarguments that you successfully overcame will recreate the dynamic tension that maintained your own interest. It will maintain your reader's interest, too.

11. FACE YOUR READER. This is the master rule that includes all the others. Facing your reader means that you stop mumbling to yourself and start adopting a "communicative attitude." Once you do this, you will adopt the other ten rules instinctively and automatically.

I might add a twelfth rule: don't go on and on. Emphasis is fine but redundancy can be a bore. Don't tell your reader more than you can reasonably expect him to want to know about your subject.

3 ✍ *Woo Your Reader*

The Myth of the Captive Reader

You have a large vocabulary, handle words well, and have no trouble writing a clear, well-constructed sentence. Why, then, is so much of your stuff so hard to read? The major reason may be that you are writing to a captive reader, someone whose job it is to read what you write and whose attention, therefore, you are taking for granted.

Captive readers do exist, of course. They are professional people who must keep themselves informed of the latest developments in their fields; teachers reading their students' papers; maintenance engineers and technicians at the mercy of manual writers; bureaucrats soliciting responses; and citizens receiving communications from their government. Employees receiving memos from management and management getting information from their employees, both are captive.

The list can be expanded almost at will. But in reality the idea of the captive reader is a myth. It is a myth because readers, like all people everywhere, yearn for freedom and rebel against captivity. They do this by taking revenge and tuning out, by failing to get the writer's message.

In the case of the teacher having to read a paper that takes him for granted, his conscious or unconscious resentment will express itself in his grading and his attitude toward the student. In the case of professional people writing to an audience of captive peers, they will be less successful than they could be in gaining acceptance for their ideas and adding to their reputation. The maintenance engineer may just give up on the maintenance manual and try the hit-and-miss approach, risking the possibility of compounding equipment failure; or ship the gear back, or leave it unused, or waste hours and hours in fruitless efforts, all because the writer did not take enough trouble to communicate.

Even in the management-employee relationship, the proprietary attitude toward the reader can backfire. Employees, too, tune out. They don't get the message, they misinterpret, they ignore, and they forget. Proper communication is one of industry's biggest problems.

On every level you can see captive readers rebelling by erecting barricades of indifference and boredom. To breach these walls you have to enlist their interest. You have to treat them as equal partners in the two-way enterprise of communicating. You have to stop treating them as captives. What it involves is not changing your sentence structure or improving your score on a readability scale, but changing your attitude toward your readers.

Examples

The "captive" version on the left is a manufactured example. On the right is how Charles Darwin, in his book **The Voyage of the Beagle,** *actually phrases the report.*

Evidence independently and separately corroborated by (a) the aforementioned juvenile apprehended by Mr. Low and (b) the previously referenced individual identified as Jemmy Button, points to the unavoidable conclusion that under the circumstances of severe food deprivation during the winter period, the native inhabitants evidence a preference for elimination of their tribe's female senior citizens to that of their canine population. Interrogated upon this subject, the subject youth stated that the canine population was capable of catching otters, whereas the senior females were not.

From the concurrent, but quite independent evidence of the boy taken by Mr. Low, and of Jemmy Button, it is certainly true, that when pressed in winter by hunger, they kill and devour their old women before they kill their dogs: the boy, being asked by Mr. Low why they did this, answered, "Doggies catch otters, old women no."

The next example gives two versions of a simple editor-to-author memo.

"Captive" Version

Recommended Version

To: Author, Metric Measurements
Subject: Abbreviations in Tables
Reference is made to Chapter 14, titled Tabular Work, Paragraph 14.4, of the United States Printing Office *Style Manual*, Revised Edition, January 1967, which states that "To avoid burdening tabular text, commonly known abbreviations (see rule 10.48, p. 159, and rules for abbreviations) are used in tables. Metric and unit-of-measurement abbreviations must

Dear author:
All units of measurement spelled out in your tables will be changed to their abbreviated forms, in conformity with our style guide.

be used with figures." Table 4–5 of your manuscript submitted to this office for final edit shows the unit of measurement, i.e., meters, spelled out instead of abbreviated as "m." Inasmuch as the style guide ruling our editorial functions incorporates the GPO *Style Manual* by reference, author's permission is requested to change this matter accordingly as indicated.

Here is an excerpt from a grant proposal:

"Captive" Version	Recommended Version
3. There are three degrees of Dis-ability/Handicap Limitation. a. Persons with severe lack of social opportunities and/or the most limiting disabil-ities. 85,000 in L.A. City; 20,000 institutionalized. b. Persons with pronounced lack of social opportunities and/or pronounced limiting disabilities. 199,000 in L.A. City. c. Persons with some lack of social opportunity and/or some limiting disabilities. 284,000 in L.A. City.	3. In the city of Los Angeles, we have three degrees of handicap limitation due to disability: a. Severe—85,000; 20,000 insti-tutionalized. b. Moderate—199,000. c. Mild—284,000.

The following paragraph, taken from the work of a well-known political scientist, is an example of the almost total obscurity that can be parlayed into the reputation for brilliance and originality that the author does indeed enjoy:

These uncertainties do not rule out the necessity for deciding which power structure to favor. But they do increase the short-term significance of modes of behavior and related aspects when deciding which conditions of action to promote or discourage in the interest of order. In the case of regional expansionism, the means with which expansion is promoted can be more or less incompatible with order. This aspect is important in itself. But it is even more important in relation to a second aspect: whether the target of an expansionist drive is a viable entity or only an artificial creation that is apt to provoke endless upheavals as long as it exists. A crucial, if not always self-sufficient, test of viability is the capacity to resist pressure. Some modes of pressure are, however, less conclusive than others; those which depress the standards of international relations are by and large the least conclusive. It is too simple to argue that the political regime unable to withstand subversion is unfit to survive because it lacks sophistication or support. Actually, advanced political civilizations may be the most vulnerable to subversion, while majority popular support, even where it exists, may take too long to translate into a winning countersubversion strategy.

The final example is taken from a technical manual:

Actual "Captive Reader" Approach   Communicative Approach

Operator Controls

The control panel for the 7060 subsystem contains the switches and indicators shown in Figure 3.

Power Switch-Indicator

This is a push-on/push-off switch-indicator that controls all primary power to the 7060 subsystem. The indicator remains illuminated as long as power is applied. When the switch is momentarily depressed, ac power is applied or removed from the subsystem.

Reader Controls

The tape reader portion of the control panel contains the three controls discussed below.

Start   This is a switch-indicator used to control and indicate the "automatic" mode of the tape reader. Depressing this switch causes the tape reader to enter the "automatic" mode if the RUN/ LOAD switch on the spooler is in the RUN position. The indicator remains illuminated as long as the tape reader is in the "automatic" mode.

Operator Controls (Figure 3)

Power   Push-on/Push-off switch.

Controls primary power to subsystem. Illuminates while power is on.

Reader Controls

Start   Starts tape read operation. (RUN/LOAD switch on spooler must be on RUN.) Remains illuminated during tape-read run until tape is stopped.

Stop   Stops tape. Remains illuminated, indicating availability for manual operation, until START operation is reactivated.

Tape Feed Advances tape without reading during manual operation (STOP illuminated). (Controls capstan.)

Punch Controls

Start   Starts tape punch operation. Remains illuminated until operation is stopped.

Stop   Stops tape punch operation. Remains illuminated during halt.

Stop   This is a switch-indicator used to stop tape motion by causing the tape reader to enter the "manual" mode. The indicator remains illuminated as long as the tape reader is in the "manual" mode.

Tape Feed   This is a switch-indicator used to cause the tape reader to pass tape forward (without reading) under control of the drive capstan as long as the pushbutton is depressed. This control is operative only when the reader is in the "manual" mode.

Punch Controls

The tape punch portion of the control panel contains the controls and indicators discussed below.

Start   This is a switch-indicator used to control and indicate the "automatic" mode of the tape punch. Depressing this switch causes the tape punch to enter the "automatic" mode if tape is properly threaded in the punch. The indicator remains illuminated as long as the tape punch is in the "automatic" mode.

Stop   This is a switch-indicator used to stop tape motion by causing the punch to enter the "manual" mode. It remains illuminated as long as the punch is in the "manual" mode.

4 ✍ *Face Your Reader*

The Communicative Attitude (I)

You may feel that you don't take your readers' attention for granted; that you don't treat them as captives. On the contrary, you may feel that where you err is in being too much in awe, in trying too hard to impress. You probably wish you had enough confidence to write more casually, to be a little less self-conscious. Perhaps so, but the captive-reader syndrome is nonetheless valid.

Where the captive-reader syndrome shows and makes itself felt is in your attitude toward your readers. Certainly you respect them, but do you make the effort to woo and win them? Most nonprofessional writers don't. With many it seems to be almost a question of pride. They are offering a part of themselves, the fruit of their labor; they feel that should be enough, without the endearments and the decor. And if their readers don't like it, that's too bad.

If you are one of these disdainful writers, you probably don't bother with proper titles. "He's asked the question—given the assignment—asked for the report," you justify yourself. "He knows what I'm writing about." Besides forcing your reader to supply something that you could more easily supply yourself, you are also depriving yourself of a chance to orient him to your own point of view. A well-thought-out, descriptive title will give a clear hint of the direction your answer is taking. It should work for you as the headline works for the newspaper and should not merely be an echo of the original question that prompted your writing.

Your disdain for the captive reader may show itself in your disregard of the niceties of appearance and format, almost as though these were trivial things not worthy of your attention. They're not trivial. They serve a purpose in the process of communicating, and their importance should not be underestimated.

Even more important is organization. You can organize your material so that it has thrust and will make an impact, or you can submit a passive thing that carefully avoids any overt attempt at influencing your readers.

Some writers will put readers on their mettle. "They should know this," they say to themselves. "If they don't, they have no business reading this in the first place." This attitude will express itself in the use of jargon, esoteric vocabulary, and deliberate obscurities. You'd be amazed at how many writers there are who don't really want to communicate. They're grudgingly willing to document their research and supply a record. But anything more they consider almost unprofessional, unscientific. Communicating? That's journalism. We're supplying the facts and the observations. Let those newspaper fellows popularize if they wish, but we—the scientific community—will have no part of it.

People who don't really want to communicate cannot be helped. They are content to be among the happy few functioning in an exclusive world. The trouble is that their example influences others who want to, who need to, communicate. And the first thing communicators, as distinguished from mere documentors, must learn is that they must adopt the communicative attitude. They must stop mumbling to themselves, turn away from the blackboard, and face their audience. They must get their noses out of their writing pads and look at their readers.

To repeat: it is a question of stance, of posture, of attitude. Once you assume the communicative attitude, once you try to reach out to your readers and tell them what you want to tell them, then the rest becomes easy. Not really easy in terms of doing the right things at the right times—that takes practice, thought, lots of hard work, a little luck, and a little talent. But writing becomes easy in that it stops being a painful and boring chore, because suddenly you'll find that it serves as a tool in reaching an objective: to capture your readers' minds.

Why do people really write? There is always the hope of fame and riches, but there are easier ways to win fame, and there are certainly easier and surer ways to win riches. I believe that people write and continue to write because they want to change the world a little. They want to leave their stamp on the world, no matter how humble the scope of their efforts. They want to put something into somebody else's mind that wasn't there before. They want to communicate.

Writing is an aggressive, dynamic activity. You want to attack, and you want to conquer. It isn't the sort of thing you can do with your back turned toward the opponent.

Examples

Benjamin Franklin's famous autobiography begins with a classic example of the desire to communicate.

Dear Son: I have ever had pleasure in obtaining any little anecdotes of my ancestors. You may remember the inquiries I made among the remains of my relations when you were with me in England, and the journey I undertook for that purpose. Imagining it may be equally agreeable to you to know the circumstances of my life, many of which you are yet unacquainted with, and expecting the enjoyment of a week's uninterrupted leisure in my present country retirement, I sit down to write them for you.

To which I have besides some other inducements. Having emerged from the poverty and obscurity in which I was born and bred, to a state of affluence and some degree of reputation in the world, and having gone so far through life with a considerable share of felicity, the conducing means I made use of, which with the blessing of God so well succeeded, my posterity may like to know, as they may find some of them suitable to their own situations, and therefore fit to be imitated.

The left column below is an excerpt from a government regulation that is almost impenetrable. The writer, like so many lawyers, evidently had no concern with communicating but only with nailing down all bases and covering all contingencies. The rewritten version in the right column assumes a more communicative stance and conveys the message more forcefully and clearly without losing any of the original version's information or distorting its meaning.

A creditor shall not effect for or with any customer in a general account, special bond account subject to par. 220.4(i) or special convertible security account subject to par. 220.4(j) or special action which, in combination with the other transactions effected in such account on the same day, creates an excess of the adjusted debit balance of such account over the maximum loan value of the securities in such account, or increases any such excess, unless in connection therewith the creditor obtains, as promptly as possible and in any event before the expiration of five full business days following the date of such transaction, the deposit into such account of cash or securities in such amount that the cash deposited plus the maximum loan value of the securities deposited equals or exceeds the excess so created or the increase so caused.

Prohibited transactions. Accounts affected are customers' general, special bond, and special convertible security accounts subject to paragraphs 220.4 (i) and (j) below. Creditors are prohibited from effecting any transaction which, in combination with other same-day transactions, creates—or increases— an adjusted debit balance larger than the loan value of the securities in the account. Such a transaction is permitted only if creditor obtains for deposit into the account cash at least equal to the excess balance or increase, or securities with equivalent maximum loan value, or a combination of both. The deposit shall be obtained before the expiration of five full business days following the date of the transaction.

The Communicative Attitude (II)

How do you make yourself assume the "communicative attitude"? Partly it's a question of recognizing what you're doing wrong and of stopping bad habits. Once you recognize your attitude toward your captive reader for what it is, there are a lot of things you'll stop doing because you've realized why you're doing them. But in developing a communicative attitude it isn't so much what you have to stop doing that counts as what you'll have to start doing.

How do you court and woo your readers? How do you engage their interest? HOW DO YOU HOLD THEIR INTEREST? There's no trick, no gimmick you can learn that will teach you how to be interesting, though there are a number of things you can do to avoid being boring. But before you even think of ways to interest your readers, you must come to terms with yourself over why you want to interest them, why you want to communicate, why you want to go to all the trouble of winning them, of capturing their minds as well as their obligatory time.

The *New Yorker* once had a cartoon showing the *New York Times* building with an avalanche of words pouring out of its windows and doors. There is such a torrent of words threatening to engulf us now that nobody should add to it unless it's absolutely necessary. Whenever you can do so, say it, don't write it. Nobody has invented anything, nobody ever will invent anything that can approach the beauty and efficiency of direct face-to-face contact as a means of communication. McLuhan may be right that the predominance of printed communication has passed its peak. The written word is steadily losing ground to the combination of spoken word and picture.

When we write, there should be a compelling reason for doing so. And that compelling reason must reside within ourselves. We must want to write, want to write badly enough to overcome loneliness, the desire to do more pleasant things, natural laziness, and the fear of putting ourselves on the line and exposing ourselves for what we are.

Balderdash, you'll say, what does all this have to do with my having to write that paper or report? This may be true for the poet, playwright, pamphleteer, and novelist, but what relevance does it have for the college student having to write a term paper, the engineer writing a proposal, the business administrator writing a report?

At the risk of sounding stuffy, I maintain that nobody should ever put pen to paper without a strong inner motivation, without the express desire to communicate. It simply isn't enough that somebody else wants you to write, or that circumstances compel you to write. For your writing to achieve validity, the motivation has to be within yourself.

I say this knowing full well the importance of paychecks and deadlines in stimulating creative activity. No professional writes except for the promise or expectation of money. Dostoyevsky, forever under financial pressure because of his gambling, wrote most of his novels under contract to newspapers that serialized them. He wrote the last chapters of *The Idiot* in a tremendous burst of speed, writing around the clock for several days, because he was going to forfeit a substantial amount of money from future works unless he met his deadline. Balzac wrote throughout the night, every night, because he wanted money. Ask any successful writer and he'll tell you that his reason for writing is money. But that is only part of the story. The need to communicate arises from Having Something To Say and itching to say it.

That is the real reason why people write. It should be the major, the overriding, the only reason why people write. You must have something to say. And you must want to say it badly enough to go through the labor of writing it down. Without this motivation, writing becomes a chore, a chore you'll resent and resist, and that will bear the mark of your boredom when it's finished. Writing done in this spirit will bore the reader as much as it bored the writer.

5 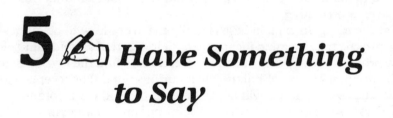 *Have Something to Say*

Once you have something to say and are itching to say it, you'll need little prompting to assume the communicative attitude. The question is, how do you find something to say, how do you develop the itch to say it when you write a routine college paper? How do you burn with that blue flame when you set out to write a report on a computer program, or a memo explaining a slippage in your schedule, or any of the other writing chores you are required to perform in your daily routine?

First of all, any writing that is mere routine should be treated that way. It is better to develop and fill in a form than to trot around the same track week after week. All other writing requirements have enough material content to bring out the communicator in the writer.

What does "having something to say" mean? The most common ingredient is special knowledge. Anything that is news is special knowledge by definition. The scientist reporting on her research is reporting news— news if she achieves anticipated results, news if she doesn't. The travel writer who tells you about lands and places you've never been to or heard about presents news. In short, any writer who reports on something that hasn't been reported before qualifies for "having something to say." It doesn't matter how humble the item is. The memo writer who announces a change in coffee-break times has something to say, as well as the letter writer who announces to his creditors that he cannot meet his obligations. On the other hand, the sermonizer who incants thoughts and ideas handed over by previous generations has nothing to say unless . . . but that leads me to my next point.

What do you do when you don't have the special knowledge that gives you something to say? What if you're not a researcher, news reporter, gossip columnist, or even an administrator? What about the college student having to write a paper on some subject that generations of college students have written papers on? What can he or she say when it has all been said before?

Perhaps you shouldn't write at all if you really feel that you have nothing to contribute. The fallacy in this assumption is your failure to realize that every writer is a unique individual, gifted with a unique point of view and a unique perspective. Writers are the sum of their experiences, and any given text, any new idea, any experience will add to that sum and slightly alter the balance. It will impinge on them in a personal way, causing a unique and personal reaction. This is what they alone, and no others, are capable of contributing.

What I'm trying to explain here is really the art of how to be interesting. A dull, prosaic mind, a mind incapable of being jarred, a timid mind closed to new propositions, a sober mind prepared to discount the joy of discovery and the disappointment of failure, the incurious mind that accepts without questioning—such a mind will never be able to produce a commmunication deserving of attention. Such a shockproof and weatherstripped mind may run with the precision of a Swiss chronometer, but it is a mechanical mind, a mind that will never be able to challenge, antagonize, convince, or inspire. A writer with a mind like that will not be interesting. He or she will not be able to communicate.

Poet and critic John Ciardi has talked about the hundreds of poems that are sent to him by individuals for review and how he goes about eliminating those that go back unread. "When a poem starts with the words, 'When I was a babe at my mammy's breast . . .' or something like it, out it goes."

What Ciardi means is that he spots a commonplace mind and he knows that such a mind will not be able to distill experience to the point where it becomes worthy of attention. Of course, prose isn't as demanding as poetry, and ordinary communications can hardly be compared with the prose written by literary artists. Ordinary communications may generate interest simply because of their message—but only if they're short. Any message longer than one or two paragraphs requires something more to make it interesting. The needed ingredient is a point of view, which we'll look at more fully in Chapter 6.

Examples

Although it should be fairly clear by now what "having something to say" means, the following examples will further illustrate the point. Each, in its opening sentence, promises a message worth reading (at any rate, to those interested in the subject).

From miscellaneous business sources:

We've had a year of record profits, but I'm concerned about possible danger signals. Foremost among these are excessive demands for credit by some of our largest customers.

The collapse of Storage Technology spells trouble for our PC production line. They've been our principal suppliers of the IBM-compatible disk drives which . . .

The PC has insufficient memory for version 3.0 of our new display software. Notice must be given to all customers that an expansion unit is needed if the program is to be run on the computer.

Unless we get an immediate infusion of cash from our parent company, we won't have sufficient funds to meet the next payroll.

*From an essay in the **Wall Street Journal**:*

Heroin's surreptitious journey to America has traditionally begun in foreign lands where its raw ingredient, *Papaver somniferum,* opium-poppy, is cultivated. But in 1979, underground chemists in California cracked the foreign connection with "designer drugs," synthetic drugs made in clandestine laboratories for pennies a dose. . . . [Six years later] the government has yet to find a way to stamp them out.

*From a report, also in the **Wall Street Journal,** where the writer implies that his intent is broader than just reporting the facts:*

A 32-year-old accident victim lies unconscious in a Florida hospital that has no neurosurgeon available. But two larger hospitals with neurosurgeons refuse to accept him upon learning that there is no guarantee his bill will be paid.

*From the **Los Angeles Times,** an economic analysis:*

The inflation news continues to be outstandingly positive, according to the reports coming out of Washington, but what we are seeing is not fully reflective of what is happening beneath the surface of the economic structure, where there are signs of at least moderate disappointment in the months ahead.

To round out these examples and show that "having something to say" isn't restricted to reporting and analyzing day-to-day events, here are Jean Jacques Rousseau's introductory lines to his autobiography:

I am commencing an undertaking, hitherto without precedent, and which will never find an imitator. I desire to set before my fellows the likeness of a man in all the truth of nature, and that man myself.

I alone. I know my heart, and I know men. I am not made like any of those I have seen; I dare to believe that I am not made like any of those who are in existence. If I am not better, at least I am different. Whether Nature has acted rightly or wrongly in destroying the mould in which she cast me can only be decided after I have been read.

Let the trumpet of the Day of Judgment sound when it will, I will present myself before the Sovereign Judge with this book in my hand. I will say boldly: "This is what I have done, what I have thought, what I was. I have told the good and the bad with equal frankness. I have neither omitted anything bad, nor interpolated anything good. . . . O Eternal Being. Gather round me the countless host of my fellowmen; let them hear my confessions, lament for my unworthiness, and blush for my imperfections. Then let each of them in turn reveal, with the same frankness, the secrets of his heart at the foot of the Throne, and say, if he dare, "I was better than that man!"

6 ✍ *Have a Point of View*

Having a point of view is not to be confused with being opinionated or prejudiced. It does not necessarily mean that you must condemn or admire, condone or reject. What it does mean is that you must react to your material. You must reflect, wonder, question, digest, interpret, condense, distill, and articulate. You must act as the filter through which the material passes.

Literally, your point of view is simply the position from which you view things. Viewing an object from above or below, from in front or from an angle, creates distortions, emphasizing some features and deemphasizing others. A flower may be viewed in a field, on a bush, or in a vase, from a short distance allowing the observation of minute details, or from a longer one giving an overall impression. Depending on your situation and inclination, you may want to stress the aroma, the color, the shape, or the setting. You may look at it with the eyes of the painter, the poet, or the lover. Your interest may be that of the botanist or that of the zoologist. You may view it from the florist's angle or from that of the hostess. You may think of its cost or anticipate its pleasure. It may lead you to speculate on the ephemeral nature of life, or on the joys of spring and summer. With a leap of the imagination, you may even look at the flower from the bee's point of view or from that of the garden pest. However you look at it, it's always a point of view—something unique that only you, the writer, can supply.

How does a point of view square with the dispassionate striving for objectivity, with the avoidance of distortion implicit in accurate reporting? It does and it doesn't. The botanist dissecting, analyzing, and classifying a flower has a distorted point of view in that he investigates aspects that are trivial to the poet or the painter. But within the framework of this basic distortion, the botanist has no difficulty remaining objective and accurate. The painter's view, on the other hand, is equally distorted and one-sided, yet equally valid. Monet spent the last decade of his long life painting water lilies, untiringly exploring their mystery, their beauty, their special fascination for his painter's eye. That was his point of view.

Your own point of view is your special way of looking at things. It is a necessity. It is also unavoidable. The good writer assumes it boldly. Timid writers try to hide it and become wishy-washy.

Having a point of view does not mean being strident or belligerent. It simply means being aware of one's own position with respect to the thing viewed. Your point of view may be dictated by your special interest (such as that of the botanist or zoologist), but even within this framework you have to assume a personal point of view by narrowing the field. Some writers find their point of view instinctively; others have to develop it, choosing it deliberately based on conscious awareness of what they are doing and what they are trying to accomplish.

How do you develop a point of view? Consider finding your point of view a discovery rather than a deliberate act. Let it sneak up on you. Let it surprise you. That really is one of the joys of writing, to find out things you didn't know were in your mind. The stumbling upon a truth. The discovery of an insight.

An insistence on understanding is the attitude required of a communicator. When you have made a discovery, then you will have the desire to communicate. You will want to share your understanding, your insight.

I find this occurring constantly, even in business and technical publications. You are faced with an opaque specification for a piece of equipment or a computer program and you gradually work your way into it, penetrating the fog of elliptic prose and careless jargon. At first, trying to untangle the knotted line of reasoning is like looking for order in a can of worms. Then suddenly you find a beginning, a thread. It may end in a hopeless knot and you may be forced to try another, and perhaps several other approaches. But suddenly you achieve a breakthrough when all the pieces fall in line and form a pattern. You understand! And this insight will be the beginning of your point of view.

Frequently the special way in which you arrived at your insight will give you your angle, the trajectory of your approach. Or your insight may give you your theme; but insight—understanding—is the one ingredient you can't do without. It may not always yield a point of view, but you won't have a point of view without it.

Your approach to your point of view will be influenced, and sometimes dictated, by your audience. Imagine trying to explain the automobile first to Benjamin Franklin, then to Voltaire, and finally to Darwin. Wouldn't you stress different aspects to each of them? Knowing Franklin's inquiring, scientifically oriented mind, you would probably go into the principles of the internal combustion engine and, of course, the electrical system, which would be of special interest to him. Voltaire, on the other hand, presumably couldn't care less. What you would stress with him would be the sociological and human implications, the extent to which the automobile has contributed to, or detracted from, the possibility of human happiness. Darwin would want to know about the ecological changes the automobile has brought about. He would want to know about smog, concrete, watersheds, wildlife, and all the other ramifications of the automotive civilization.

If you write a thesis for your professor, your point of view will be different from what it would be if you were to explain the same subject to a stranger, a friend, a colleague, your mother, or your barber. Similarly the description of a piece of equipment would differ depending on whether it was written for a maintenance mechanic or a design engineer. And a progress report could be written in substantially different versions depending, again, on who would read it.

Also, your point of view might be based on contradiction or affirmation. You contradict a widely held view, or you reaffirm one that has fallen into disrepute. You may attack a bias or defend it. In either case you will have to supply arguments to define your point of view or bolster your position. But a word of caution: Whenever you merely contradict or affirm, it becomes very easy to slip into empty verbiage and to set up your own likes and dislikes as the absolute standard of evaluation. "I don't know much about (art, painting, sculpture, music, wines), but I know what I like" is the standard pronouncement of the ignorant, smugly pleased with their confession of ignorance but unwilling to accept ignorance as a limiting factor to their ability to function as critics.

All writing is subjective. All criticism is personal. All evaluation is to some extent biased. But if you want your point of view to be respected, if you want to avoid being brushed aside as opinionated and biased, if you want to get the attention of your reader, then you must be careful to shore up your arguments with facts, figures, and close reasoning. If you have the talent for it, you may get away with the illuminating flash of wit instead of close reasoning, but such wit is rare. There aren't many Oscar Wildes among us.

Examples

Point of view is not always so clearly visible as it is in these examples, which were selected for their conciseness:

This memorandum in my sample file expresses a pessimistic point of view:

Despite a second year of record profits, I cannot join in the cheering without expressing my misgivings about some of our accounting practices that tend to conceal problems that will haunt us in the future.

New York City's Mayor Koch states his point if view about the criminal justice system in this **Wall Street Journal** *report:*

New York's Mayor Ed Koch recently voiced a common criticism of the criminal justice system. The probability of being jailed for a crime, he argued, is hopelessly low—perhaps 2% or 3%. From this he concluded that a criminal is unlikely to be deterred by the fear of punishment.

Economist Michael K. Evans, writing in the **Los Angeles Times,** *asserts his point of view about a fundamental truth:*

The theories of the economics profession haven't had much of a track record in the past few years, but one fundamental truth endures. Relative prices do count. If the price of anything declines enough, people will use more of it and less of other goods or services; if the price rises, its use will decline.

A personal point of view is expressed in this memorandum:

Based on my own experience, we can't afford to delay making a commitment on . . .

And in this report in the **New York Times:**

Move quickly. That is the first commandment according to Sir Michael Edwardes, Britain's best-known doctor for ailing corporations. It is important to act before a situation "solidifies around you," he explained. . . .

And in these two memos from my sample file:

The approach taken by this user's guide is simple. So simple that its simplicity becomes self-defeating. Most users will become impatient and want to skip ahead, only to find that they've missed important information along the way. The solution? A different way of organizing the material.

A recent study by an outside consultant concludes that our elaborate inventory control system costs more than its benefits would justify . . .

*Another from an article in the **Los Angeles Times:***

To some economists, the recommended energy and economic program is like plunging into the ocean on a cold day. It may be the fastest way to get used to the water temperature, but it will certainly make you shiver for a while. And it could give you a heart attack.

And to conclude, here is an excerpt from a brochure produced by the United States Department of Labor showing that government publications, too, have a point of view.

Workforce change is inevitable. All who deal with Manpower will benefit by a better understanding of the nature and direction of its changing patterns. To improve such understanding is the purpose of this booklet.

7 ✍️ Use Perspective

Perspective is closely related to point of view and is an element of "having something to say." You have perspective when you view something from far enough away to see it as a whole: to see the forest instead of just the trees. It is the one ingredient most often missing in technical and other types of descriptions.

Perspective allows you to view the parts of a whole in relation to each other. It lets you look at a given universe as a system where the action of one part affects the function or the state of all the other parts. Perspective implies organization. It is a wide-angle, long-distance view. You can see why it is necessary for understanding.

The oft-told story of the Indian fakir who once asked the sultan whom he was serving to commandeer five blind men and have each of them describe the parts of an elephant which he could "see" with the touch of his hands illustrates perfectly the point of perspective. The blind man who felt only the elephant's leg thought it was a tree trunk, the one who felt its trunk thought it was a boa constrictor, etc. If you see only an isolated part, you can have no conception of the whole. Unless you see the whole, see how all the parts fit together, you can have no conception of what a thing is.

You can describe an automobile engine, but without knowing what it does and what it's for, and without telling your reader how it interacts with the drive train and how the drive train interacts with the wheels, the description will be meaningless because it lacks perspective. In fiction you take perspective for granted. Without perspective, without a certain amount of distance from their subject, novelists would not be able to select, interpret, evaluate, or comment. They need perspective to perceive that all of the cogs turn only for the purpose of moving some larger entity. They must be able to view relationships and interaction; they need distance to achieve perspective.

Perspective is a built-in advantage of the writer of historical novels. He or she knows beforehand how it all comes out, puts himself into a situation that is clarified by the benefit of hindsight, and gains added perspective by being free of the emotional baggage of the present. Similarly, other writers achieve perspective by projecting their vision into the future (like Huxley, Orwell, and untold others) or by creating imaginary situations (like Swift and Butler). To get away from the odious nearness of the present, Huxley and Orwell extrapolate into the far (and not so far) future, just as Butler constructed an Erewhon and Swift a Brobdingnag as devices for viewing their own society from a fictitious distance. The ultimate use that writers make of perspective is to achieve and communicate understanding.

Substance, point of view, and perspective can all be summed up in this one word: understanding. We habitually talk about writers having a way with words; we talk about self-expression and communication, about wit and sensitivity, pathos, empathy, and humor. We admire brilliance of mind and elegance of phrase. I don't quarrel with any of this. But what we generally fail to acknowledge is this very simple thing that distinguishes the artist from the plodder, the writer from the hack: the compulsion to understand. This is the driving force behind all true writers, no matter how great or how modest their ambition.

We come across this need for understanding, and this lack of understanding, every day. We talk to doctors who don't listen, to lawyers who know the answers before we ask the questions, to officials who don't really want to hear our story. We fight bloody wars and conduct lacerating feuds because we hear only our own voices and fail to hear and understand the problems of our antagonists. We prolong strife because we don't listen and don't want to listen.

Recently an acquaintance settled a long-standing feud with his stockbroker. He had one understanding of the situation, his broker another.

He tried to explain his side to the broker's administrative manager, but without success. The man had already made up his mind and didn't listen. My friend eventually talked to someone else who did listen and then, in one sentence, explained why he was wrong. The explanation completely satisfied him. The second man had listened and tried to understand what had bothered my friend, whereas the first had lacked all desire to listen and understand. He already knew. He didn't have to put his knowledge to further scrutiny. Knowledge to him was a quantifiable, definable, packageable thing. Knowledge was following procedures step by step. It did not encompass understanding.

This attitude, of course, blocks any attempt to communicate, any attempt to create a channel between two minds. Without understanding, without a willingness to listen to, and perhaps anticipate, the questions arising in your reader's or respondent's mind, there can be no communication in the true sense of the word.

Note

It is difficult to cite examples of perspective in the form of isolated sentences or paragraphs without distorting the writer's point of view and making him appear moralizing and philosophizing. It is equally difficult to show a lack of perspective without artificially devising something that would be ludicrous. The use of perspective is, after all, a matter of process. It is something that is pervasive, something that makes itself felt in the whole rather than in fragments capable of being lifted out of context and held up as examples.

8 ✍ Find a Theme

The word "theme" comes from the Greek and means literally "something laid down." In other words, you lay down a statement and move it forward to where it can be viewed and considered. In music a theme is something you can whistle or hum: the composer states it, develops it, abandons it temporarily, comes back to it, and plays with it until he is finished with it. In writing you are rarely quite so explicit. To avoid being obvious, you may even go to some length to hide your theme, but whether you let it show or not, the theme must be present in a piece of writing just as it must be in a piece of music.

You might say that theme is related to point of view as a dent is related to the impact that has caused it, or as steam is to heat. All three of these pairs are in a causal relationship. One part of the pair is the result, the other the cause.

To get a feeling of the real meaning of theme you can try an experiment. Get together with a group of friends and write down in one sentence your unconsidered responses to various one-word stimuli: love, marriage, work, sex, teenagers, campus militants, etc. Try it. You'll find it both amusing and instructive. I have seen prosaic, sober, middle-aged people—bookkeepers, housewives, accountants, administrators—come up with one-sentence responses that had the wit, grace, and compactness of polished epigrams. It is important to allow a very short time limit for the response (not more than one minute) to obtain instinctive, spontaneous reactions. Once you pause to reflect and consider, the internal censor takes over and something gets lost. You will then write not what you think, but what you think you ought to think.

What you say in these one-sentence responses is the statement of a theme; something that sums up your individual point of view. It will give you the opening line, the point of attack, for an essay and in some cases even for a report.

But theme is more than just a beginning. It is also the glue that holds the pieces of a report together. It is the unifying element, the cohesive force without which the parts of a piece of writing fall apart, getting lost and scrambled in the reader's mind.

When you know your subject well and seem to be in control of your material, it becomes easy to forget the need for a theme. This is particularly true when you have more than enough material to work with. An embarrasment of riches, a glut of wealth, frequently causes a writer to lose sight of the unifying theme and thereby to lose coherence.

This happened to me the first time I attempted to condense the material in this book into a half-hour lecture. The difficulty wasn't so much a question of boiling the material down as of structuring it into an organic whole. After stewing for a few hours, I finally realized that I needed a theme. Once I became aware of the need, it was fairly easy to analyze my material and discover my theme: the need to be interesting. Having found my theme, I could now jot down an outline without further difficulty, following essentially the same points as those of Chapter 2. What finding my theme did for me was to give my presentation an organic unity it did not have before. It fused the disparate parts into a whole.

Harping on a theme can be overdone, too. Writers have been known to drag in theme whether it fits or not, rubbing the reader's nose in it, so to speak. Institutional promotion, for example, frequently becomes quite self-conscious in its search for a theme. In the heyday of the conglomerates, reports to stockholders would often cling to farfetched themes like the glories of Greece and the quaintness of medieval and Renaissance commerce. Here the dragged-in themes presented an opportunity for stunning color photography; but they also were clever devices for hiding the thematic emptiness of the companies the reports represented.

Theme is often prominent in expositions and trade fairs, where it is used to key advertising and coordinate merchandising. Magazines may devote entire issues to a single theme, and some writers their entire lives. Theme is point of view made explicit, and also point of view made pervasive. Whether you select a theme deliberately for commercial or other utilitarian reasons, or play on one because it holds you captive, it must be present—even in your outline.

Examples

The threat to American industry is the theme sounded in this excerpt from the New York Times:

No one seems certain exactly when, but some time last year, for the first time, the United States began to import more electronic products than it was selling abroad.

A somber theme—the horror of war—is sounded by the editor of National Geographic:

Half a world away from our Vietnam Veterans Memorial stands a macabre monument to the same Southeast Asian war, a wall of 9000 nameless skulls—all removed from one mass grave—all from people murdered long after the United States pulled out—all victims of a war that began in the dim past and continues to this day.

The impact of personal computers on managers is the theme of a Fortune article:

Skeptics used to greet pioneering motorists with the cry, "Get a horse." People who dismiss the impact of the personal computer, including many of the folks who use the machine, tend to employ the phrase, "It's just a tool." Some tool. The personal computer is already working profound changes in the lives of businessmen who use it, though few are aware that anything very significant is going on.

Optimism is the theme of this memo:

Our industry has been depressed for so long, an upswing in demand appears to me as all but inevitable.

From a market letter:

If we could predict next year's fashion in stocks, we could buy them now and make a lot of money in a short time. But fashions are not predictable and we don't attempt to do so. Instead, we will be satisfied if we can *identify* fashions *after* they begin to take shape.

A direct quote by the subject states the theme of this article on architect/ designer/film-maker Charles Eames in the journal **Gambit:**

"I think that this, in a sense, is the objective: to get many of the rewards of life from the work that you do."

An article on handicapped children by Mary Glockner states its theme in these words:

When you're working with a handicapped child, it is important to think of him first of all as a *child*, more like other children than different.

In a paper dealing with data management in the social sciences, delivered at the 15th International Technical Communications Conference, writer C. Ray Funkhouser of Stanford University takes for his theme the unavoidability of imperfection:

The social scientist must somehow obtain valid, reliable, and quantitative data in spite of the fact that his subject of study—people—is the most elusive subject there is. Although improvements in approaches, methodology, and data-handling are being made all the time, it is unlikely that predictions made by social scientists will ever be perfect. But then, what is?

"Professionalism" is obviously the theme of James G. Shaw in a paper delivered at the same conference, from which this example was culled:

"I'm not a publications engineer or a technical specialist in publications," a candidate for a job half-growled at me. "I'm a writer. I write. You name it; I can get your message across." In other words, he was telling me that he was a pro.

In another paper from the conference, the writer, Dr. Elise Sisk, states her theme as well as labels it:

My theme will be how to exploit the advantages inherent in being an in-house teacher and how to offset the disadvantages.

As used by politicians, thematic emphasis can easily degenerate into rhetoric. Here, to conclude, is a borderline example written by Senator Ted Kennedy, from a book titled **ABM:**

There is no priority higher than that of guaranteeing our national security and safety. Without an effective military force, and without a worldwide understanding that we have the unwavering will to use this force when our national interests are in danger, we unnecessarily place our way of life in danger.

9 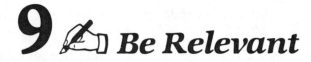 Be Relevant

At least as important as theme is relevance. The word "relevance" has been overused in recent years, but I can think of no other word that could take its place. Relevance is a relational term: it expresses the relationship between subject and object—writer and reader. The degree of relevance is the degree to which the reader feels personally involved with the material.

Even though relevance—or relevancy—may be inherent in the subject matter itself, it is the writer's responsibility to make it clear why the subject is relevant to the reader, in other words, why it is important to him. How does the writer establish that link with the reader, that needed bridge between two minds? This is not always easy. It may require empathy, imagination, insight, and a lot of hard thought.

Why and how is the thought of Plato or Aristotle important—relevant—to today's college freshman, after a lapse of two-and-a-half millennia and astounding changes in population and technology? Why and how is Shakespeare relevant to the mathematics major or engineering student? Why and how is the Bill of Rights relevant to the shop steward in a factory? These questions must be faced by teachers, writers, and speakers. They cannot be glossed over; they demand answers. Without an answer, without the necessary bridge to the reader's or listener's mind, the substance of these subjects will evaporate. The message of Shakespeare or the Bill of Rights will fail to make an impact.

In most cases the task of establishing relevance will not be quite so difficult. More often than not it will be simple. In business and professional communications it will usually be satisfied with an opening phrase like "the purpose of this . . . is . . ." But beware of adopting this or a similar phrase as a formula. Used in this way, any phrase quickly becomes drained of content because the writer may stop thinking about the real purpose of his message. He may fall into the habit of thinking that his purpose is to inform, whereas the reader may not be interested in being informed. Figuring out why something should be important to the reader always requires thought. Don't ever forget that you are attempting to take away some of your reader's most precious commodity: his time. If you want to get it, along with his attention, you have to give him a reason for giving it to you. And that reason can only be either his implicit confidence that anything you write is important—and few writers are in a position to command this kind of respect—or his speedy recognition that what you are writing about is relevant; that it represents a solution to some problem that concerns him.

Examples

The following introduction (left column) to a community college Shakespeare course is drivel, totally irrelevant either to the student bent on acquiring practical knowledge or to the one interested in an education. The rewritten version on the right might be more successful in establishing the relevance of Shakespeare to both types of students.

William Shakespeare is generally recognized as the greatest poet of the English language. Every educated person should have a knowledge of his works. Most of the most frequently quoted phrases are quotations from Shakespeare's plays. His mastery of words and the richness of his vocabulary are astonishing. It isn't always easy to read his plays because many of the words he uses are no longer in current usage, but the effort is richly rewarded by the pleasure of understanding the gorgeous music of his language. We can also learn much from the "bard of Avon" about human nature and human emotions. Reading Shakespeare is a truly enriching experience. The opportunity to receive guidance in discovering the beauties of our great-

A group of young Navy men visiting London was steered by a service club to a stage performance of Shakespeare's *Romeo and Juliet.* At the conclusion an 18-year-old sailor from Nebraska was heard to shout, "O Shakespeare, you old son-of-a-bitch." Purists may be offended to see the bard apostrophized in this manner, but the enthusiasm and emotion behind the exclamation speak louder than the scholar's critique. Shakespeare is as alive today as he ever was. No playwright is performed as much, no poet read as thoroughly. No passion is foreign to him, no corner of the heart too secret for him to enter. And the power of his imagery and magic of his language remain fascinating no matter how often a passage is heard or read.

est poetry should be welcomed by all who wish to acquire an education.

All this does not mean that it is easy to love or like Shakespeare. The very richness of his language presents difficulties; the subtlety of his mind poses enigmas that remain debated and unresolved to this day. It takes effort and guidance to come to grips with his work. But the rewards are there—if only in making one wiser and more perceptive to the quirks and foibles of the world.

From an unsolicited proposal, in which the writer shows relevance by defining the nature of the problem and the size of the potential market:

Wild animals are tracked routinely by tiny radio transmitters attached to their bodies. Why not children, hikers, and others at risk of getting lost? Each year, millions of people expose themselves or their children to this risk. Every summer children walk away from picnics and get lost, instigating a frantic search—one that is unfortunately not always successful.

We have developed and patented a prototype device suitable for this application and will grant exclusive marketing rights . . .

From a memorandum attached to an employees' attitude survey:

. . . The reason why we have commissioned this study is to obtain reliable information that will enable us to make changes, if needed.

From another memorandum:

We have a video tape of remarks made at the last stockholders' meeting by our Chairman and Chief Executive Officer, Mr. Charles McKellar. His remarks are of importance to every member of our staff. They provide a new perspective on the direction in which the company is moving and will give us fresh enthusiasm for the work we're doing and personal goals we're pursuing.

The tape will be shown . . .

*The next example, from the introduction by Walter Sullivan to Charles Darwin's **The Voyage of the Beagle**, explicitly establishes the relevance of Darwin's travel book to modern man's view of himself:*

This book was prelude to what became probably the most revolutionary change that has ever occurred in man's view of himself. The change, in fact, has still not fully run its course. It demands that we regard ourselves as inseparably a part of nature and accept the fact that our descent was from more primitive creatures and, ultimately, from the common origin of all life on earth. It is the view that we will never fully understand ourselves until we understand our origins and the traits—chemical, biological, and behavioral—that we share with other species.

The authority of an act of Congress is used to establish relevance in this next example from the Preface of the **GPO Style Manual:**

By act of Congress the Public Printer is authorized to determine the form and style of Government printing. The *Style Manual* is the product of many years of public printing experience, and its rules are based on principles of good usage and custom in the printing trade. . . . Essentially, it is a standarization device designed to achieve uniform word and type treatment, and aiming for economy of word use. . . .

A final example, from a Symposium on "Values in Contemporary Society" held at the Rockefeller Foundation, shows how Professor Irving Kristol uses a historical approach to show the importance—relevance—of his topic to contemporary society:

The problem of technological power and man's use and abuse of this power is not a new problem. The Greeks thought about this carefully. Medieval Christianity thought about it carefully. The Jewish and Islamic traditions thought about it carefully and profoundly. We have much to learn from them—not just to use them as illustrations, but really to learn from them.

---

10 ✍ State the Problem

The major reason anything is important to anybody is the existence of a problem, and the best way for a writer to stimulate his readers' interest is by defining and stating his problem.

Herbie Miller was a delightful baby and his parents did not worry when he didn't say so much as "mama" by the time he was two years old. They became a little concerned when he still didn't speak at age three, and panicky when he remained silent at age four. Their doctor told them not to worry. "Herbie is a perfectly healthy child. All his reflexes are okay.

He'll start talking when he's good and ready. Einstein started talking quite late, when he was just a little younger than Herbie."

At six Herbie still didn't talk and his parents were in despair. Could he be autistic? Was he retarded? What was wrong with Herbie? A psychiatrist observed him for a number of weeks. No, there was nothing wrong with Herbie. He was a normal, healthy, happy child. He just didn't want to talk.

At seven Herbie came to the breakfast table one morning, took one sip of his chocolate and spat it out. "This stuff is awful," he told his mother. "It's cold and bitter."

"Herbie, you can talk," his mother beamed. "I'm so glad you can talk. How come you've never said anything before?"

"Up to now," said Herbie, "up to now everything's been okay."

With apologies for the old story, the point is, there's no point in communicating unless there is a problem. There has to be a problem to arouse people from their lethargy. It is up to the writer to perceive, define, articulate, and respond to his readers' problems if he wants to awaken their interest. Good writing, all good writing, is problem-oriented.

Taken in its widest sense, there is a problem lurking in some form or shape behind every piece of writing, whether it's a newspaper column, a novel, a play, or a technical manual. Information alone is meaningless unless it is related to some need or desire to know. The need to know reflects the existence of a problem.

The problem may be stated explicitly or implicitly, but it is always there. It may be presented in the form of a question (e.g., "What can we do about smog?"), or as an answer ("Steam-driven cars will end smog"), or as a denial of a proposed solution ("Battery-powered cars are no answer to the smog problem"). In great works of literature the problem may be so subtle, so hidden and obscure as to defy any clear-cut, unambiguous interpretation. But in whatever form or shape it is presented, readers must be aware of the problem so that they will be interested and go on reading.

Check your newspaper to see if it isn't true that just about every item and article either deals directly with a problem—taxes, the Mid-East, corruption, decisions and rulings affecting private and public interests— or fills a desire or need for knowledge—science news, gossip, local events.

When you deal with straight information, it is particularly important to bear in mind your readers' specific curiosities, their "problems." You must fill their need to know, but before you can do this effectively you must first determine *what* they want to know and why they want to know it. You must, in other words, understand your readers' problem; or you may have to make them aware that a problem exists to which you have a solution. A solution needs a problem as badly as, or worse than, a problem needs a solution. You can have problems without solutions, but you can't have solutions without problems.

The problem is the crux. The writer must always be aware of it, whether he states it in so many words or leaves it implicit.

Examples

From Hamlet:

To be or not to be, that is the question.

From the "History of an Infantile Neurosis" by Sigmund Freud:

Here then . . . are the riddles for which the analysis had to find a solution. What was the origin of the sudden change in the boy's character? What was the significance of his phobia and of his perversities? How did he arrive at his obsessive piety? And how are all these phenomena interrelated?

From a report in the Los Angeles Times:

Although the death rate in the United States has declined in recent years, a newly completed report shows that the rate in Los Angeles County is 53% higher than the national average and that the gap seems to be increasing.

From an article in the National Geographic:

The biblical cycle of fat years followed by lean years appears to have come true again in the terrible drought and famine that now grip Ethiopia and other countries south of the high dam on the Nile at Aswan.

From a business letter:

Our principal supplier of IBM-compatible disk drives has gone into Chapter 11 and we're actively looking for a reliable manufacturer capable of supplying us with a portion of our disk drive requirements.

From a financial report on Xerox:

Xerox's systems group was given a difficult task when it was created in El Segundo two years ago. After a series of disappointments, the company's prospects were at their dimmest, and the 5000-employee group was charged with devising new products and charting a new strategy for selling a cluster of products called office-automation systems.

From a market letter:

Despite the strong recovery, prices of many commodities—copper, gold, lumber, rubber, cotton, and others—have been sliding for four months in a row. Some economists have interpreted this unexpected weakness as a signal that investors are selling off real assets because they fear a general fall in prices and wages—in a word, deflation. That hasn't happened since the Great Depression, when deflation was followed by economic collapse.

*Coming from an organization dedicated specifically to investigating and solving problems, the reports of the Committee for Economic Development offer a rich source of examples: The problem is "resistance to change" in this example from **Innovation in Education:***

The future of the schools depends in large part on whether they can overcome in educational policy and practice what is frequently an extreme conservatism and a strong resistance to change.

From *Improving Federal Program Performance:*

The notion of inefficiency in the federal government is well established in the popular mind. Even Presidents share this view of government. Yet voters, Congressmen, and Presidents continually act to increase the federal establishment's activities and responsibilities. Resolving the paradox of the government's present level of effectiveness and its growing assignments has become a vital national issue.

From *Reducing Crime and Assuring Justice:*

The interest of the Committee in crime and justice stems not only from the economic fact that crime costs the business community an estimated 16 billion dollars a year and boosts prices paid by the consumer. Far more important, crime undermines the very basis of American society. It creates fear and destroys the mutual trust and confidence which are the foundation of a healthy nation.

From Chapter 3, *"Attaining High Employment without Inflation," Fiscal and Monetary Policies for Steady Economic Growth:*

Most people agree with the objectives of high employment, stable prices, steady economic growth, and a satisfactory state of the balance of payments. Serious questions have been raised about the compatibility of these objectives.

Opening paragraph of *Trade Policy toward Low-Income Countries:*

The economic condition of the low-income regions of the world is one of the great problems of our time. Their progress is important to the high-income countries, not only for humanitarian and political reasons but also because rapid economic growth in the low-income countries could make a substantial contribution to the expansion and prosperity of the world economy as a whole.

11 ✍ Be Responsive

Closely connected with problem-awareness, and equally important, is the need to be responsive to your intended reader's expectations. In other words, don't give him apples when he's expecting oranges. Since your reader will have these channelled expectations only when he himself solicits a response, it seems self-evident that you will not be effective if you disappoint these expectations.

It should not be necessary to emphasize this point, but nonresponsiveness is such a widespread failing that it must be stressed. Reports, business letters, proposals, exam essays—all these frequently suffer from nonresponsiveness.

Some years ago a study conducted by Hughes Aerospace Corporation showed that the overwhelming reason why their losing proposals lost was that these proposals were unresponsive to the needs of the customer. Metaphorically speaking, they proposed battleships when the customer needed tugboats, Cadillacs when he required Jeeps. And vice versa. In other types of writing the correlation between responsiveness and success or failure isn't as easy to detect as it is in proposals, which either win or lose, but it exists all the same.

Examinations and term papers, for instance, are notorious for frequently "missing the point," which is another way of saying that they are unresponsive. Students don't read the questions properly; they don't analyze them; they don't ask themselves, "What is the problem that requires an answer?" They may write beautifully, but what they write may be the answer to the wrong question and all but worthless from the point of view of responsiveness.

Failure to analyze and understand the question, failure to interpret the problem correctly, is the major reason for failure to communicate. It is again the failure of understanding that results in the breakdown of communication.

The most frequently encountered example of unresponsiveness is, of all things, the computer. People who have trouble with computerized billing find themselves stymied in trying to tell the computer that "it" has made a mistake. They return the bill with a polite note, which the computer can't read, and in due time the computer spits out another bill with the same mistake. This has been known to go on for years.

But people can be as unresponsive as computers. "Programmed" to do things in a certain way, some people start to whirr madly when this secure routine is threatened—that is, when they're expected to respond in any way different from the one they're grooved in. Also, people generally don't pay attention. To illustrate the point, play this game with a group of friends and acquaintances. For best effect, the group should be fairly large. Prepare and duplicate a long set of instructions that you ask them to follow. Begin with some perfectly straightforward, routine questions like name, address, age, etc. Then come instructions on how to fill in the rest of the questionnaire, including a statement that everybody should read through to the end of the form before filling in any of the blanks. The last sentence of the form reads, "Don't execute any of the previous instructions. Put down your pencil and wait quietly until everybody else is finished." In between these two key instructions can be included anything wild you can think of: "Run three times around your chair"; "raise your arm and hold it up for five seconds"; "draw a quick sketch of your neighbor." You'll find it amusing to see how many people will do all these things because they failed to "read through to the end." You should also stipulate some time limit, so that everybody can get into the proper racing spirit.

Unresponsiveness is a snag in all communications, but it is particularly noticeable in proposals. Suppose you are the head of a fund-raising firm and receive a Request for Proposal from the National Foundation for the Preservation of Our National Resources (a fictitious group). This group wants to raise funds to make it possible to lobby in Congress, to file injunction suits against industries posing a threat to the public's resources, to make emergency land purchases, and to publicize the dangers of pollution and erosion. How would you respond to this request? Would you stress your awareness of the existing environmental problem to show that you are completely in tune with the foundation's aims? (This is what a large number of my students did when I gave them this problem in class.) Or would you deal with the foundation's immediate problem: "How do we raise the money?" The foundation already knows about the problem of spoilage, pollution, and waste. What they need is money, and that is where they need your help. To be responsive you have to demonstrate a plan for raising money.

People frequently fail to see the obvious because they are programmed by their expectations. In most cases the predictable reaction is good enough. The actual head of the fund-raising firm, unlike the students in class, is conditioned to give the proper response. Training and conditioning will elicit a statistically satisfactory sample of correct responses in all cases. But if you want to place yourself outside the bell-shaped curve of statistical predictability, then you must become aware of the need for looking at problems with fresh eyes, for being responsive. It is the mark of the effective communicator. It is the mark of the writer.

Examples

Scientific Computer Corporation has requested proposals for the sale or lease of a fleet of automobiles for its executives, sales personnel, and customer service representatives. This is a first-time venture for Scientific Computer, since in previous years the company reimbursed its employees for per-mile use of their private cars. Shown below are two sample responses (with address, signature, reference, etc. omitted).

Thank you for requesting us to propose on a fleet of automobiles for your executives, salesmen and service personnel. I would urge you to consider the Cadillac for all three types of users. As you know, there isn't a finer and more prestigious automobile made in this country than the Cadillac. In supplying your personnel with such an outstanding motor car, you will not only reap the benefits each individual derives from driving one of the finest motor cars in the world, but also garner the immense prestige associated with the Cadillac trademark. On fleet purchases, we are prepared to allow you discounts ranging from 15 to 25 percentum below list price, depending on total number of cars delivered.

We regret that we do not lease cars; all our sales are outright. We will be happy, however, to help you arrange financing at advantageous terms.

The lack of responsiveness in this letter is obvious. The Request for Proposal should not have been sent to these people in the first place, since they are obviously not in the right business, though a more energetic, or hungrier, businessman could probably have found a way to make a proper response. The writer of the following response did:

Thank you for requesting Carfleet Sales to submit a proposal for supplying a fleet of automobiles suitable to your needs. We have carefully analyzed your requirements and have reached the following conclusions:

1. *General Economic Considerations.* Appendix A is a reprint of an article in *Fortune* magazine that compares the cost effectiveness of reimbursing employees for the use of their privately owned cars versus maintaining a fleet of company-owned, and in some instances company-maintained, automobiles. As is graphically demonstrated in Figure 3 of this article, actual cost savings begin to accrue at point C of curve 4, and point F of curve 6. Both of these curves bear a close resemblance to your own requirements, curve 4 to those for sales personnel and curve 6 to those for service personnel. Your projected usage in each case is well beyond the break-even points C and F. Similar economies cannot be projected for your executive automobiles, but we assume that your rationale in this case is not purely economic but directed toward providing your executives with additional perquisites.

2. *Lease/Buy Decision.* On the basis of the financial and use data you have given us, we recommend that you lease your fleet rather than buy it. We

enclose in Appendix B a number of computer runs based on different sets of projections for tax rates, profits, interest rates, labor rates, and cash flow. All these projections are highly tentative, but since the consensus in our industry definitely favors leasing over outright purchasing, our analyst concurs that this would offer you the greatest advantages despite your current favorable cash position. Appendix B also shows the analyses on the basis of which we recommend a two-year lease period for your customer service personnel. One-year periods are recommended for your salesmen and executives who should drive the latest model at all times.

3. *Service Contract....*

4. *Types and Makes of Cars.*
    a. Executive Cars. Inasmuch as our own dealership contract does not enable us to supply your executives with the type of luxury automobile you specified in the RFP, we have entered into a partnership agreement with Superb Motorcar Company....

12 ✍ *Select Your Point of Attack*

Where to Begin

Beginnings are crucial. How do you begin to tell your story? At what point do you penetrate your readers' armor of indifference? How do you engage their interest and make them want to go on?

There are no easy answers, no absolute rules. You can begin with a question, with the statement of your theme, or with a statement of the problem. Or you simply begin with answers found and conclusions reached.

In reports and memos, a summary of conclusions is generally the best beginning. It gives your readers an idea of where you're heading and how you're going to get there. It orients them, points them in the proper direction, and arms them with the right expectations. It prevents them from getting lost and becoming frustrated.

Have you ever tried to put a jigsaw puzzle together without a picture to guide you? It can be done, of course, but it isn't easy. Reading is a little like assembling a jigsaw puzzle. Having a conception of the finished product makes the job of reading a report much easier. It gives you a clue to where each piece of information fits.

A surprising number of writers avoid this helpful practice, saving their conclusions until the very end. As a report editor I've found that one of my most important functions is to switch last paragraphs and sentences to the beginning. Frequently this is all that is needed to put an unfocused piece of writing into proper focus.

Stating your conclusions first and following up with supporting evidence is the natural and straightforward way of presenting an argument. Doing it the other way around is a sign of being insecure and hesitant. It may lend an aura of judiciousness and objectivity, but it is a false aura, borrowing its gloss from pseudo-scientific method, misapplied and misunderstood.

Science since the days of Galileo and Newton has been based on inductive reasoning, a method by which you achieve generalizations from observing specific instances. Observation of falling bodies led to the formulation of the law of gravity. Induction is the accepted method of observation and discovery, but it is a slow and cumbersome method of transmitting information. The scientist is, after all, guided by intuition in making the observations that lead to discoveries. Lacking this intuition, the reader needs some kind of illumination to lead him through the maze of observations. This illumination can be provided by an assembly picture—the summary of conclusions.

The method of conveying information by starting out with a conclusion is called the deductive method. It is the method used in everyday learning and thinking, and it should be used by every writer who cares about reaching his reader's mind. Failure to use the deductive approach is probably the one fault most responsible for causing confusion and inducing boredom.

An example of inductive writing is the trip report given in strictly chronological order. Another example is the test report that starts with test run A and proceeds through run N before presenting any kind of conclusion. To spin out a story is one thing if you are a talented story teller able to tell it with charm, wit, and humor. Only a few enviable people have this talent. But it's quite another matter to hold up the conclusion of a story or report in the mistaken belief that you must save the best for the last, forcing your reader to stay with you to the bitter end. It usually doesn't work that way. Few readers are captive enough to go along.

Most people are quite unaware that they are writing in an inductive pattern. The temptation to marshal all arguments before stating the conclusion is so great that most writers succumb to it without a struggle. Even after you've become sensitized to the pitfalls of inductive writing, you have to check from time to time to make sure that you haven't fallen back into old habits. Setting out all the evidence before you reach the verdict seems to be the proper, the scrupulous thing to do; but it should be avoided. An inductive structure in informative writing is the implacable enemy of clarity, and it kills interest.

Structurally the inductive pattern resembles a pyramid resting on its broad base of evidence and building up to its fine point of conclusion. The deductive structure, conversely, resembles an inverted pyramid. All the weight of evidence and argument presses down on its point to achieve maximum penetration.

Besides its intuitive and logical advantages, the deductive pattern has been proved to be more effective. When two sets of the same material, one set written in an inductive and the other in a deductive pattern, were presented to two equal groups, the group exposed to the deductive material scored far higher in comprehension. The only change in most cases was simply that the last sentence was switched to the first sentence, making the paragraph deductive instead of inductive. You'll also find that the deductive structure appears to be shorter than the inductive, which in itself is a considerable advantage.

Few rules exist that are always right. You can probably dig up examples where an inductive pattern is preferable to a deductive one, but I don't think these examples will be easy to find. I do believe that a deductive structure will benefit most writers in most cases and that every writer should at least be aware of the severe drawbacks inherent in an inductive structure.

Examples

In addition to the examples of the problem and theme statements shown in preceding chapters, all of which could also serve as "points of attack," the following show other types of openings used in different circumstances. All, however, use a straightforward, deductive approach that goes right to the heart of the matter. (See also Appendix B for a further example.)

*From the business section of the **Los Angeles Times:***

Visa International and MasterCard International joined seven banks Monday in filing a multi-million dollar lawsuit in U.S. District Court here against an illegal credit card racket. They say thousands of people were tricked into revealing their credit card numbers by phone to "boiler room" solicitors.

Walt Disney Productions, citing a marked turnaround in its filmed entertainment unit, reported that earnings and revenues for the year's second quarter and first half were the highest in its history.

Storer Communications said Monday that it has spurned a buy-out offer and instead will begin an offer early next week to buy 3 million, or 18%, of its own shares outstanding.

From an obituary:

Former Sen. Sam J. Ervin Jr., who symbolized to the nation a latter-day Diogenes bent on finding the truth in an era of Watergate lies, died Tuesday in a Winston-Salem hospital.

From an environmental newsletter:

The impact of traffic on the environment is of such major importance that to ignore it would be irresponsible.

From a business letter:

We regret that we are unable to respond to your request for proposal on . . .

From the introduction of **Social Responsibilities of Business Corporations,** *published by the Committee for Economic Development:*

This statement deals with the social responsibilities of business enterprises in contemporary American society. It is intended to contribute to a clearer view of these developing responsibilities and to show how business can best respond to the changing requirements of society.

From Chapter 1 of John Stuart Mill's **On Liberty:**

The subject of this Essay is not the so-called Liberty of the Will . . . but Civil, or Social Liberty: the nature and limits of the power which can be legitimately exercised by society over the individual.

What about Anecdotes?

I once asked a magazine writer friend to help me edit a technical report on an automatic fare collection system for the London Transport Board. He livened up the introduction with an anecdote about an American who wanted to go to Knightsbridge Station and kept ending up at Tottingham Square. I laughed but regretfully crossed it out. Amusing anecdotes have their place, but not generally in a technical report. On the other hand, no discussion of beginnings and opening paragraphs would be complete without at least a mention of anecdotes. They are the single most important "hook" in feature articles, and may occasionally be useful even in essays and reports.

A feature article in *Scientific American* may be written by a reputable scientist and based on thorough research, but the author intends the article for an informed and educated lay public rather than for his professional colleagues. He is writing something that is—from his point of view—more superficial than a report on the same subject written for a scientific journal.

A feature article is by its nature impressionistic, an essay is philosophical, and a report factual. In a feature the anecdote is used to quickly illuminate a point that would otherwise have to be explained laboriously in broad and general terms. For example, in a biographical feature it is far easier to bring your subject to life by narrating an anecdote than by trying to describe his character in general terms. Finding an anecdote may require a lot of digging, but it is worth the effort. Anything you find can usually be used for your purpose. The significance depends entirely on your own interpretation. If it illustrates the specific point you want to make, so much the better. If it does not, you can treat it as the exception that confirms the rule. For example, if you want to stress your subject's habitual and fanatical promptness and come across the one instance where he was late for an appointment, you can perhaps use his embarrassment as a peg on which to hang your story.

Anecdotes are particularly valuable when you are writing about people because the things you can say about people are by their nature imprecise. Our vocabulary is not rich enough to cover the wide range of nuances that differentiate people's behavior. An anecdote bridges the language gap by illuminating a generality with something specific. But anecdotes need not be restricted to writing about people. For example, in an article about inertial navigation systems, you might begin with an anecdote about the crew of the *Nautilus* breaking into cheers at the precise moment when the instruments indicated that their submarine was crossing the North Pole under the icecap. This would illustrate the ability of inertial navigation equipment to operate without the availability of external navigational landmarks. We should bear in mind, however, that this kind of an anecdote is useful only in an article for the general public, unfamiliar with the principle of inertial navigation. It is useful, in other words, in an article *about* inertial navigation. It would be useless and redundant in a report directed to engineers. Such a report would in all likelihood focus on a specific development in the field of inertial navigation, and the impressionistic approach of an anecdote could therefore be counterproductive.

In a feature article, the value of the anecdote can hardly be overstressed. I remember a feature article, reprinted as sales promotion material and probably written for that purpose, that went a long way in persuading me to buy a certain car. The article was built around an anecdote about a near accident two test drivers had when they got drunk and went sailing 150 feet through the air but landed safely and continued their wild ride. It threw a spotlight on the car's roadability, sturdiness, and safety, illustrating the point the writer wanted to make about the car.

If your anecdote is humorous and can provoke a smile and a chuckle, you have breached your reader's indifference and you are that much ahead of the game. But an anecdote need not be funny; it can be sad, sober, and even tragic to illustrate the point you want to make. The value of the anecdote is always that it substitutes something specific for a generalization. You can talk about a car's sturdiness and roadability and have me nodding politely but hardly paying attention. But if you tell me about a car sailing through the air and landing safely, then I'll sit up and take notice.

If you can't dig up a suitable anecdote, you may have to invent one to generate interest as only the specific can do. This is done all the time by professional writers and is not in any way reprehensible as long as your story is merely apocryphal and not a deliberate lie. And unless the story you invent is detrimental to your subject, no objections will ever be raised. But the anecdote you invent must be plausible. That is, it must be something that could have happened, even if it did not actually happen.

Digging up an anecdote is one thing; writing it up is another. Again it is difficult to establish rules on how an anecdote should be written. Generally it is best to keep it short and crisp. Don't waste too much time setting the stage, and don't hold off too long before making your point. A single paragraph is usually enough to tell your story, but if your material is thin, you may have to spin out the anecdote and let it become the heart of your story. Also, writing an anecdote is difficult and you may have to write and rewrite it to get it in shape. But the satisfaction you get from writing a polished, finely honed paragraph is worth the trouble.

Note

Abraham Lincoln told of seeing a man who was holding an elephant by the hind legs. "What should I do if the elephant should try to run away?" the man asked. "Let him run," Lincoln answered.

In trying to give examples of anecdotes I feel like that man with the elephant and am inclined to take Lincoln's advice just to let it go. All literature, ancient and modern, is filled with anecdotes, and you can even find them in the writings of philosophers and natural scientists. Dr. Mungo Parks, an 18th century traveler who was commissioned to explore and write a report on the geography of unexplored portions of Africa, proceeded to write one long chain of arresting and fascinating anecdotes. Similarly, Charles Darwin's *The Voyage of the Beagle* consists to an overwhelming extent of anecdotes. And although anecdotes have only limited use in expository writing, they can be used in some instances—for example, in this book at the beginnings of Chapter 1, Chapter 10, and this chapter.

13 ✍ Organize—Then Outline

You've done your homework, have a point of view, and have gained insight, perspective, and understanding. What's the next step? That old standby, the outline?

The need for outlining is probably the most oversold item in the grab bag of advice dispensed to writers. Some people call it the blueprint, as necessary to construct a piece of writing as it is to build a house. Maybe it works that way for some writers, but I don't know any of them. An outline, as I see it, is a tool of communication—something you may need to convince somebody that you know what you're doing; something you may need to get the assignment or go-ahead. An outline may even help you direct and focus your own thinking, but it's not usually a blueprint.

Following an outline is basically uncongenial to writing. It tends to staunch the natural flow of ideas and break the dialectical tension that alone can carry both writer and reader through to the end. Outlining is analytical, writing is integrative. Writing gives form—*Gestalt;* outlining breaks down the whole into its components. Yet we are indoctrinated from grammar school on to outline before we start to write, an emphasis that has probably done more to spoil potential writers than it has to help anybody learn to write.

Nevertheless, there are certain types of reports for which you must have an outline, and there are some outlines that will serve as blueprints. I shall discuss four types of outlines: the responsive, the selling, the coordinating, and the categorical, and how none of these should be confused with organization.

The Responsive Outline

When you accept an assignment to write a report, the person who gives you the assignment acquires a legitimate concern for your work. He becomes responsible for it inasmuch as he has delegated his task to you. He has a need and the right to know how you are going to proceed. Your outline is your response to this need.

The outline need not necessarily be complete or firm. In most cases it will merely serve as a base, subject to change as the work progresses. But it will be a tool of communication between you and your client or employer; it will provide a necessary basis on which you can agree or disagree; and it will give you, the writer, the invaluable benefit of feedback. Should you happen to be on the wrong track, it will be easier to change your approach at the outline stage than after you've gone so far and so deep that any change becomes major surgery. On the other hand, if you are on the right track, approval of your outline will make writing easier by boosting your morale. But the most important function of this type of outline is that it eliminates misunderstandings.

The Selling Outline

The selling outline is the one you use to get an assignment. Even if your credit is high, it will ease both parties' minds if you write an outline in which you summarize any conclusions and list the topics you intend to cover, possibly a one- or two-sentence summary for each. If the report is to be the end product of a research project, you may find it difficult to write an intelligent outline before you have gone fairly deep into your research; but you'll probably have a good idea of the nature of the problem you are going to investigate, of alternative approaches available, and of the results you expect to obtain. A statement summarizing these points will constitute your outline.

This kind of outline, actually more a proposal than an outline, can be highly useful. It will clarify your own thinking by forcing you to come to grips with the problem and serving as a checklist of what you have to do to complete the project. It will reassure your client that you're on the right track, that you know what you're doing and are not going to waste your time or his money. It will help him make up his mind, if his prior commitment is needed.

The Coordinating Outline

The coordinating outline serves as an instrument for coordinating several writers on one project. If an outline is necessary in the two-way relationship between writer and client or employer, it becomes doubly so in the case of a cooperative effort. Without it there might well be chaos. In large projects initiated by governmental agencies, for example, the requesting service or agency usually supplies detailed and mandatory outlines specifying precisely what subjects are to be covered, where, and in what depth. Ordinary report requirements are usually less stringent, but whenever multiple authorship is involved, the need for some kind of an outline is self-evident, if only to keep individual authors from invading each other's territory. Ideally, this outline will correspond to the table of contents of the final report.

A good method of coordinating multiple authors in planning and writing large proposals and reports has been developed by J. R. Tracey and others at Hughes Aircraft Company, at Fullerton, California. The method is called "storyboarding" and is based on three concepts: every subject, no matter how large and complex, breaks down naturally into information passages of roughly 500 to 1,000 words; each of these passages should be treated in modules of equal length (one two-page spread), including a rough sketch for an illustration and a strong statement of the topic thesis at the beginning; and these modules should then be developed as "storyboards" and assembled into a wall display, pinned to the walls of a room where they become available for group review.

The prime advantage is high visibility. Everybody involved in the proposal can see at a glance what everybody else is doing, get an idea as to the status of the project, and see where it is heading. A second advantage is flexibility. The storyboard modules can be revised, replaced, combined, or shifted around until the proper strategy of presentation has been achieved. A third advantage is the discipline it imposes on the writers, who are forced to think in terms of small modules, strong thesis statements, and illustrations.

A typical storyboard is shown in Fig. 13–1. The size of each storyboard is normally 11 by 17 inches.

The Categorical Outline

The categorical outline is more a format specification than a vehicle of communication. Categories include such headings as Introduction, Summary, Summary of Conclusions, Statement of the Problem, General Description, and Detailed Description. They serve the purpose of giving a necessary degree of rigidity and structure to your thinking and can be useful if each category is fleshed out with one or more sentences sketching its content, but they should not be confused with what is frequently referred to as the "organization" of the material.

Organization

Webster defines "organism" as "a complex structure of interdependent and subordinate elements whose relations and properties are largely determined by their function in the whole," and "organize" as "to arrange

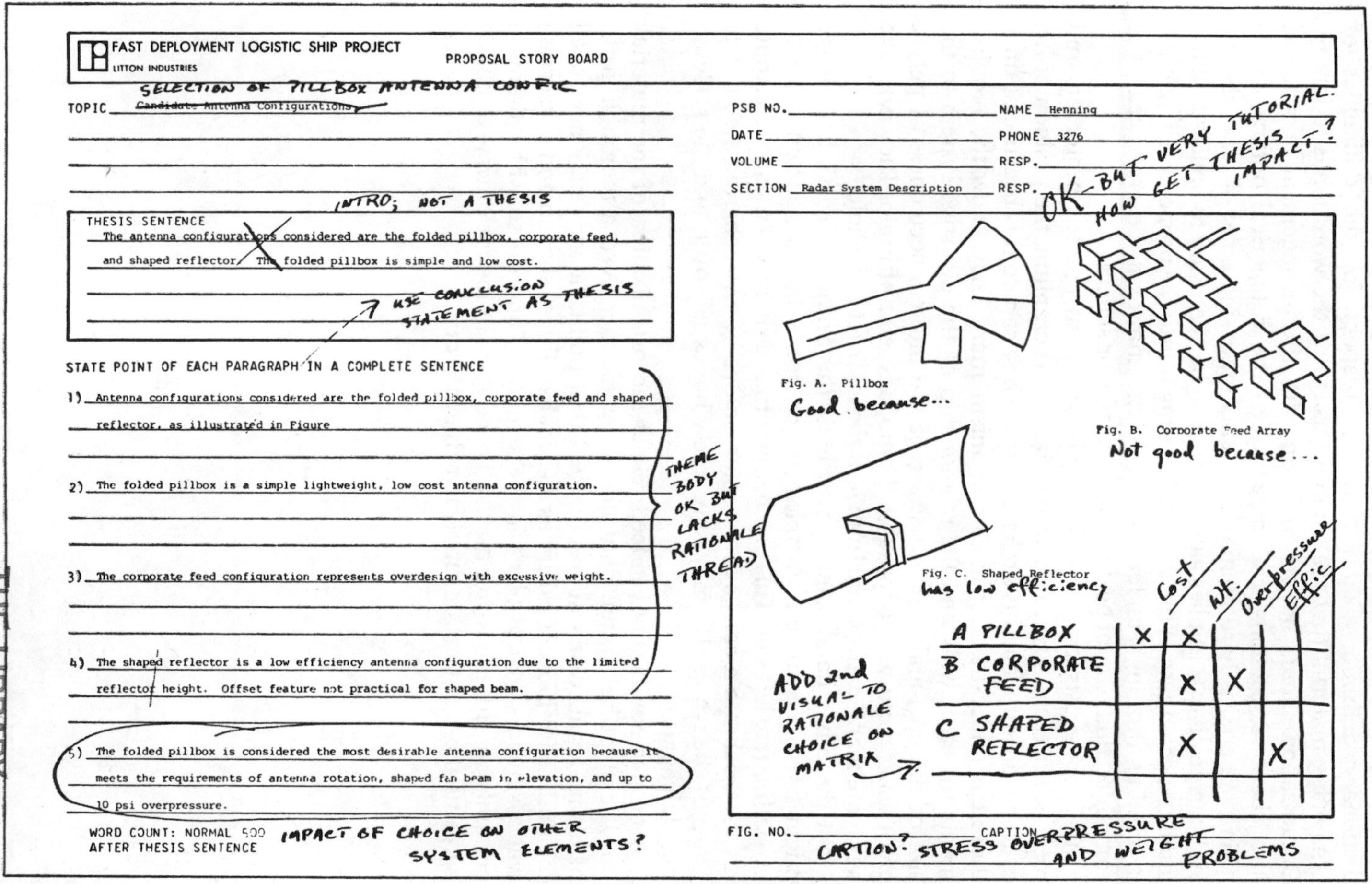

FAST DEPLOYMENT LOGISTIC SHIP PROJECT   PROPOSAL STORY BOARD
LITTON INDUSTRIES

TOPIC ___ SELECTION OF PILLBOX ANTENNA CONFIG. (Candidate Antenna Configurations)

PSB NO. ___
NAME Henning
DATE ___
PHONE 3276
VOLUME ___
RESP. ___   *VERY TUTORIAL?*
SECTION Radar System Description
RESP. ___   *OK BUT VERY THESIS?*
RESP. ___   *OK. HOW GET IMPACT?*

INTRO; NOT A THESIS

THESIS SENTENCE
The antenna configurations considered are the folded pillbox, corporate feed, and shaped reflector. The folded pillbox is simple and low cost.

USE CONCLUSION STATEMENT AS THESIS

STATE POINT OF EACH PARAGRAPH IN A COMPLETE SENTENCE

1) Antenna configurations considered are the folded pillbox, corporate feed and shaped reflector, as illustrated in Figure ___

THEME BODY OK BUT LACKS RATIONALE THREAD

2) The folded pillbox is a simple lightweight, low cost antenna configuration.

3) The corporate feed configuration represents overdesign with excessive weight.

4) The shaped reflector is a low efficiency antenna configuration due to the limited reflector height. Offset feature not practical for shaped beam.

5) The folded pillbox is considered the most desirable antenna configuration because it meets the requirements of antenna rotation, shaped fan beam in elevation, and up to 10 psi overpressure.

IMPACT OF CHOICE ON OTHER SYSTEM ELEMENTS?

WORD COUNT: NORMAL 500 ___ AFTER THESIS SENTENCE

Fig. A. Pillbox   *Good because...*

Fig. B. Corporate Feed Array   *Not good because....*

Fig. C. Shaped Reflector   *Was low efficiency*

Overpressure   OK   Eff Lo   Cost Lo

	Overpressure	Eff	Cost
A PILLBOX	X	X	X
B CORPORATE FEED		X	
C SHAPED REFLECTOR		X	

ADD 2nd VISUAL TO RATIONALE CHOICE ON MATRIX

FIG. NO. ___   *CAPTION: STRESS OVERPRESSURE AND WEIGHT PROBLEMS*

Fig. 13-1. A typical storyboard module. (Courtesy Hughes Aircraft Company)

THE LIBRARY
U.A.M. DRAWER 3599
MONTICELLO, ARKANSAS 71655

or form into a coherent unity or functioning whole: integrate." These dictionary definitions show a decent respect for the difficulties of organizing material that the common usage of the word tends to ignore. Organization should not be confused with the arrangement of material into chapters, sections, and paragraphs—the categorical outline. Organizing material is hard mental labor encompassing point of view, theme, and perspective; it implies gaining the insight necessary to understand the interconnectedness of the data and putting it into the proper relationships; it requires thorough understanding of the matter to be organized; it is something that cannot be done by rote, rule, or schema.

Anthropologists can take the jawbone of an ancient protoman and reconstruct from this fragment the size of his cranium, the position of his eyes, his posture, and his skeletal frame. They can do this because of their thorough understanding of the organism man. They know the requirements for erect walk and the relationship of the digestive system to the size of the jaw, and they are aware of the interconnectedness of pelvis, erect walk, hand with opposable thumb, and size of brain. They can take a fragment and extrapolate from it to reconstruct the whole.

On the other hand, someone without the anthropologist's knowledge might try to assemble a complete set of bones into a skeleton and end up with a few left out. This can happen to a writer who tries to distribute his material into a categorical outline before he has achieved a complete grasp of the whole. He may have a few bones left over, and the skeleton may fall apart.

A proper outline does indeed reflect the organization of the material, but it cannot be written until the writer has achieved a thorough grasp of his material. When he has reached that point, he may no longer need the outline for himself except as a checklist. Every section and subsection will assume its logical place in the structure, and do so with minimum compulsion. But the writer may still need the outline for others—to obtain agreement or consent, or simply to achieve order.

14 ✍ Develop Thrust

Three Recommendations on Style

To reach its target and accomplish its mission, writing must have thrust. It must be able to make an impact. Essentially, this driving force must be generated by your desire to communicate—your communicative attitude—but you can carry out the desire by stylistic attitudes such as preferring personal pronouns to awkward third-person circumlocutions, using the active voice rather than the passive voice, and choosing verbs instead of nouns.

Personal Pronouns: I, We, and You, or It and They?

You can write forcefully and well without ever using "we," "I," or "you." But you should not hesitate to use a personal pronoun if it fits the situation.

Many writers frown on the use of personal pronouns in formal, business, and institutional writing. It's hard to see why. When we write, we don't address ourselves to institutions. We write to and are read by real people. At its best, writing is a poor substitute for the warmth and intimacy of direct personal contact. It is an indirect form of communication that incorporates many advantages but is, nevertheless, a substitute. Why then should we add to the inherent sterility of the substitute by aggravating the formality and dehumanizing the act of communication?

There will be times when we have no choice. We may be required to use the formal third person by the rules of an employer, the idiosyncrasies of our readers, or the requirements of a specification. But when there is a choice, I would strongly recommend the use of the personal pronoun.

Some years ago I worked on a proposal that was managed by John H. Rubel, who had formerly been Assistant Secretary of Defense, Research, and Development, one of the most important jobs in military procurements. The proposal was directed to the Navy, and more specifically to an admiral known for his austerity. The man who wrote the style guide for this proposal recommended a formal approach: We will always refer to ourselves as "Litton Industries." "Not so," came back Mr. Rubel's emphatic reply. "We will always refer to ourselves as 'we.' " If the man who had passed on billions of dollars of procurement didn't know, who would? (P.S. The proposal won.)

Aside from warmth and directness, the personal pronoun will sharpen your sense of responsibility. The institutionalized third person gives you a psychological out—a mask to hide behind. This is no longer possible when you have to say, "I did so and so," or "we performed such and such." If you did the work, you deserve the credit—or you may have to take the blame. Either way, using personal pronouns will make your writing job easier. All circumlocutions consume time and energy. The third-person circumlocution can drain both writer and reader. Particularly annoying are indirect approaches like "it is felt," "it is believed," and "the company conceives of." How much easier and pleasanter it would be to use the personal pronoun in all of these cases!

All this is not to say that you should push yourself into the foreground and use the personal pronoun where it has no business being used. For example, if you describe a thing, there is no reason why you should inject yourself into the description. An account of the procreative cycle of the housefly doesn't gain by a narration of your personal disgust for flies; nor is a description of Mt. McKinley improved by your personal sense of awe.

The immodest tendency of some writers to personalize things that should remain objective probably accounts for the disdain and disrepute that personal pronouns have fallen into. "Place yourself in the background" is valid advice, given by most writers on writing. If your subject interests you enough for you to write about it, then your enthusiasm, your theme, and your point of view will make themselves felt whether or not you describe your own reactions. Using the personal pronoun may in this case be immodest and inappropriate, distracting the reader's attention from the subject matter. But if your own observation, your own work, your own ideas are part of the substance of your subject, then by all means avoid the awkward circumlocution and use the personal pronoun.

There is also a myth that use of the third-person pronoun somehow enhances objectivity. "The XYZ phenomenon was investigated" seems to have a more objective ring than the straightforward "We investigated," or "I investigated." This is nonsense. It took a person, not a machine, to do the investigating and no apologies are needed. And the personal pronoun is as valid in the abstract as it is in the body of the report. Most scientists as well as writers on scientific reporting today share this opinion.

From a purely technical point of view, you'll find that using "I" or "we" makes your writing more forceful for the simple reason that it compels you to use the active voice.

Prefer Active Voice

Use the active voice whenever possible. This is not a rule. It is a recommendation. In many instances the passive voice may be better, if not unavoidable (see Chapter 23, "Passive Voice," in Part Two), but usually the active voice will give your writing a drive and vigor that passive construction would destroy. Look at your newspaper for examples of active-voice writing. Here are samples, picked out almost at random: "The margin of the vote *sends* a message to the President that . . ." "Forty Republicans *joined* 208 Democrats today . . ." "If the events of the past week *prove* anything, they *prove* . . ." "They *laid* their lives on the line." "Thousands of illegal aliens *poured* across the borders to their homeland today." "Spend a Buck *wins* the Kentucky Derby . . ." "They *built* Hitler a mighty military machine and dutifully *defended* this madman." "The Russians *loosed* a terrible vengeance." Any of these sentences could be restructured in the passive voice and would probably be written that way by self-conscious writers trying hard to be correct, formal, and objective. Experienced writers addressing themselves to millions of readers know that they have to be lively, forceful, and direct if they want to hold their audience. Without exception, these writers prefer the active voice.

The active voice also makes it easier to construct a simple declarative sentence having a subject, predicate, and object. When you use the passive voice, the object becomes the subject and is acted on instead of being the actor. For example, "A message to the President was sent by the margin of the vote" is flabby. "The vote sent a message" is direct, simple, and unambiguous. The active voice gives a structure to your sentences that the passive voice tends to hide.

Cultivate Verbs

The active voice invites the use of verbs because verbs describe action. Look at the italicized verbs above. All of them are action verbs that propel the mind forward. They characterize and give meaning to the subjects of their sentences. Verbs are the backbone of all good writing. Yet bureaucratic writers manage to avoid using them with remarkable ease. (See Chapter 24, "Vitiated Verbs," in Part Two.)

15 ✍ Be Specific

Details Are Necessary

I've been harping at length on the need to be specific but find it very difficult to give specific reasons and specific examples that would prove my point. The generalization is unquestionably the highest attainment of the human mind and it would be foolish to try to put it down. Newton's formulation of the laws of thermodynamics was a generalization, as was Einstein's general theory of relativity. The enlargement of the human mind is based on its ability to generalize, to go from the particular to the general, to abstract rules and formulate laws. The difficulty is that this ability and this drive reside in relatively few of the highest minds, and that the rest of us tend to confuse generalities with generalizations. Generalities, unlike generalizations, usually are trite and uninteresting.

Success in the marketplace is not in itself a measure of value, but it is a valid measure of the interest a piece of writing is able to arouse. And on this basis it can hardly be questioned that the specific wins hands down over the general. What accounts for the abiding "success" of the Bible? Is it its moral teachings, or is it its wealth of drama and detail of human interest that have inspired writers, painters, and sculptors throughout the centuries, giving them a wellspring of source material that never seems to dry up, remaining fresh and interesting despite untold repetition? Even in our own unreligious times, biblical source material regularly finds its way to the top of the best-seller list: Thomas Mann's tetralogy *Joseph and His Brothers;* Gladys Schmitt's *David the King;* James Michener's *The Source;* and Irving Wallace's *The Word*, to name just a few. Familiarity and repetition have never yet dulled our fascination with the very human tales in the Bible. This fascination is never dulled, that is, as long as it is whetted by the expectation of some new detail, the discovery of something new and specific we had been unaware of.

Shakespeare's works have been called the mirror of mankind, not because of brilliant generalizations but because of his insight into details and specifics of character and behavior. George Bernard Shaw is the prime example of the playwright mainly interested in ideas—generalizations. But the success of his plays is due not so much to the provocativeness of his ideas as to the vitality of his characters. His plays are about people, not ideas. For example, his views on English accents are ultimately less interesting to us than are his characters, Eliza Doolittle and Professor Higgins.

We thrive on details and yawn over generalities. We may become intrigued with a new fact that is stated in general terms, but we'll quickly lose interest unless that general statement is fleshed out with specific details. The amount of detail wanted will vary with each individual, depending on his prior familiarity with the subject, his education, and his willingness to learn. On some subjects, I may want to inform myself at the level of detail given by some standard, unabridged encyclopedia; on other subjects, the sketchier and more general information given by one of the encyclopedias written for schoolchildren may be quite adequate for my needs. But I won't go to an encyclopedia in the first place if I don't want a degree of precise, detailed, factual information.

One reason why generalities are boring is that they usually betray the writer's lack of understanding and knowledge of his subject. The writer who thoroughly understands his subject won't dream of fobbing you off with vague and general statements about its nature. The lazy writer who hasn't done his research will describe his subject in general terms because he doesn't have the knowledge to describe it in specific terms. He'll be content to describe a man as good or bad without giving details of behavior that would prove one or the other.

This does not mean that a writer should altogether avoid the interpretive generalization. This remains perhaps his most important writing function. But the specifics must follow if the generalization is not to lose validity and the reader's interest. It is also a question of credibility. Few writers can get by on authority alone; most have to prove their point. They can do this by reasoning, backup data, other types of precise details, and examples. Later chapters deal with how to present arguments, statistical material, and descriptive details. Little need be said about how and when to cite examples other than to recommend strongly that you do so frequently. "For instance" and "for example" are magic words that liven up any piece of writing. They introduce some specific detail amplifying a previous generalization.

16 ✍ Wrestle with Yourself

There Can Be Conflict in Technical Reporting

Everybody agrees that conflict is the prime mover in drama, the short story, and the novel. Even in the essay, the conflict of opposing ideas is fairly obvious. But can we expect to find conflict in a technical or business report?

A report is supposed to be objective, presenting problem, evidence, and conclusion. It is not a polemic, not a thesis, not a philosophical essay. Here are four typical situations:

1. You are managing a project employing X number of people whose salaries are paid for by an outside contractor. Your task is to report on progress accomplished.

2. You have studied a certain problem and report your findings.

3. You have investigated ten potential suppliers and report your evaluation.

4. Your team of engineers has developed a new type of automobile engine and your report describes this engine.

Where in all this can there be conflict?

There is none if you view reporting as a mechanical function, more akin to recording than to communicating and interpreting. But the conflict in all four of these reporting functions becomes apparent when you change your attitude from that of recorder to that of spokesman-communicator.

Objective reporting is a myth. It's a widely believed myth, but a myth all the same. Fair reporting that avoids undue distortion and gives consideration to opposing viewpoints is a goal all reporters should keep in mind, but truly objective reporting does not exist. You are not a camera. You are not a recording machine. You are the one who points the camera and places the microphone, the omnipresent editor who continually exercises judgment in selecting one facet for reporting while rejecting another. You may be an impartial observer, but it becomes difficult to the point of impossibility to be a totally impartial reporter.

As a reporter, by the nature of your function, you must condense, delete, emphasize, deemphasize, expand, select, and reject. You must, if you function properly, interpret. You may try to be objective, but you will not succeed in suppressing your individuality. You are like the anonymous letter writer who tries to conceal his identity by changing his handwriting but who cannot change it enough to fool the handwriting expert; or the forger of a painting who cannot consistently imitate the master's brush strokes to the point of escaping detection. You, the so-called objective reporter, are the filter through which everything must pass. Like any filter, you too will change the thing passing through you; that is, you will ever so subtly change the information you have gathered.

The referee at a boxing match may come close to complete objectivity in giving points to one or the other of the two fighters. But the same referee functioning as reporter after the fight—perhaps being interviewed on television, or talking about it with friends over a beer—will no longer have, or attempt to have, the same degree of objectivity. He'll interpret, using phrases like "I thought," or "it appeared to me that," or "Joe connected more often but his punches didn't seem to have the same effect as Willy's." Even as referee he was more than a recorder; he used judgment. All the more would you expect judgment from the far more deliberate act of written reporting.

If you agree that objectivity is a myth, you may still wonder where the concept of conflict may possibly enter into report-writing. Conflict is the struggle to prevail against opposing forces. Viewed in the proper light, every report represents that kind of struggle. In the example of the progress report, your purpose is to convince the contractor that the work they're paying for is being done to their satisfaction, that difficulties and delays you have encountered are justifiable, that you are approaching anticipated results, and that their continued confidence in your performance is warranted. If you fail to convey this general impression, the contractor may cut off funding and cancel the project.

In the second example, where you have studied a problem and report your findings, the inherent conflict is implied by the word "problem." Problems exist only where there are opposing forces. Your report will have a built-in conflict factor.

The third example deals with the evaluation of ten potential supply sources. Again, a strong conflict element is inherent in the subject matter. Ten suppliers are in competition for your patronage. In evaluating them, you will weigh the strong points and the weak points of each of them and base your decision on a rationale that in itself will be the vector product of competing forces such as quality versus cost, elegance versus reliability, delivery capability versus product performance, etc. A shoot-'em-up horse opera has no more conflict than this situation.

Finally, in the case of the new automobile engine, would your company have spent millions of dollars to develop a new engine type if it was not an improvement over the old type? Would you write a report if all the results were negative? The questions answer themselves. The forces in conflict in this report are classically simple: the new clean engine defeating that old devil, the smog-producing internal combustion engine.

Of course, you'll also have to give a description of the new engine, and it is in the descriptive parts where most reports tend to fall flat. This need not be so.

In a dictionary, a technical manual, or some other type of reference work, definitions and descriptions should be presented as concisely, soberly, and factually as possible without any attempt to make them forceful and dynamic. Reference material claims no one's attention. It must be there when it is needed, but it isn't read as a continuous text, since each definition is a self-contained item, written to be absorbed as a discrete unit. The tension created by conflict is, therefore, unnecessary and usually undesirable.

But a report is a different type of document serving a different purpose. In a report, anything that can be dissected into discrete units, whether they be procedural steps, physical characteristics, or performance characteristics, should not be given in the form of a narrative description at all but should be tabulated, as in a manual. The discussion, however, is a different matter. Here you give the tradeoffs, the pros and cons, the reasons why a certain procedure was adopted and certain steps added or omitted, the significance of one performance characteristic versus another, etc. The discussion should be mostly argument, an exposition of conflicting forces. Conclusions reached—the results of the discussion—are tabulated.

The technique used for presenting an argument is the ancient one of rhetoric, or more specifically that of dialectics, which is the art of reasoning about matters of opinion in conformity with the laws of logic. In its simplest form, dialectical argument proceeds from thesis to antithesis to synthesis. Dialectics are frequently compared to the swing of the pendulum, but this analogy is misleading. A pendulum swings in a plane and gradually loses force. Dialectical argument feeds on itself, spiraling toward a climax before achieving resolution.

Anything that exists in time demands an end in time. It must promise resolution—but resolution following climax and achieved in stages, not immediately. It is the goal, the end toward which all action—and all dialectical writing—must be directed.

Implicit in the concept of a goal is that of direction. And implicit in both is the need for a propelling force. Goal, direction, force—these are the elements of narrative writing. They are the elements of all natural phenomena.

An electrical circuit is the connection between a voltage potential—the force—and ground, the point of resolution. A direct connection between voltage and ground would be a short-circuit, serving no purpose and lacking all interest. A true circuit drops its voltage, its force, across one or more resistances—a light bulb, an electric motor, a heater element, etc. These resistances are the conflict elements of the circuit, the intermediate reference points by which the circuit can be observed and described. The circuit has force, direction, conflict, and resolution.

The opening chord of a symphony generates a degree of expectancy, setting up a force, a tension in the listener. In musical terms this happens because the chord is not yet "resolved." The final resolution will occur with the last chord of the symphony, the one by which it is generally known and identified. This last chord will not be sounded until forty or fifty minutes after the first, and during all this time the composer will have maintained the arch of tension by not going in a straight line toward resolution but constantly building up tension and only partially resolving it until the final resolution of the last chord.

On a proportionately more modest scale, a similar need exists for building and resolving tension in expository and narrative writing. The usual way of generating the propelling force in narrative prose is to state a controversial premise, deny an accepted one, or raise a question. Check any newspaper or magazine article, or anything else written to hold your attention, and you'll find that the opening statement falls into one of these three categories: the premise denied, the premise affirmed, or the premise questioned. Any one of the three will put you in a slightly argumentative frame of mind, creating enough tension to make you want to go on.

In the next paragraph the writer will usually reverse his field, citing some of the arguments that can be made against the opening arguments. These counterarguments are then further qualified, counterqualified, and so forth until the question is wrung dry and the resolution achieved.

What the writer does, in fact, is to set up an oscillation paralleling those that can be observed in all natural phenomena. This is an almost instinctive process, practiced automatically by all who write unless the instinct is artificially inhibited by learned misconceptions about the nature of expository writing. It takes deliberate effort to damp the oscillations, but it is astonishing how many writers do make the effort.

Without the oscillation, without the dialectic of ideas, the mind is drowned in monotony. It can persist for only so long in one direction before it feels the need to reverse. Continuation beyond that point then becomes counterproductive, weakening rather than reinforcing the mind's absorptive capacity.

The telltale words and phrases at the corners of the dialectical switchbacks are connectives like *but, although, however, on the other hand, nevertheless, by contrast, contrary to*, etc. These words signal to the reader that the direction of the argument is being switched, allowing him to assume the proper mental posture before he is confronted with the evidence. Without these directional signals, the reader may be puzzled over the meaning of one thought following the other without a connecting bridge.

A writer who thinks dialectically rarely needs to remind himself to put in the dialectical connectives. They will suggest themselves naturally. He may be more likely to use too many and may have to make an effort to suppress them from time to time. The important element is again that of stance, of posture. The writer who wants to win an argument cannot turn his back to the reader.

17 ✍️ *Read It Aloud*

If writers made a habit of reading aloud what they wrote in silence, there might be no need for books on writing. It's the kind of discipline that will make you cut, prune, and rewrite, no matter how pleased you were with your silent draft.

It is even more productive if you read aloud to a live audience. You may be able to fool yourself with the sound of your voice, but this becomes more difficult when you get a direct response—or no response—from an audience. The experience can be painful. If it is, you've gained a great deal as a writer. Was it de Maupassant who read all of his stories to his cook? If for no other reason, it's a pity that kitchen help has become so rare these days. Try to select an audience with no literary pretensions. If they don't get your message, there may be no message worth getting.

Most successful writers are also superb readers. Truman Capote had a high-pitched, squeaky voice, but when he read one of his stories, he held you in the palm of his hand. You forgot the voice; you forgot the looks; you listened. A good writer knows how to communicate, on paper or by voice.

Reading aloud will give you better perception not only of pacing and word usage but also of sentence structure.

The sentence is your basic building block. No, that's a bad analogy. A building block is something that's square, even, and uniform. These are three qualities you'll want to avoid in any series of sentences forming a whole. But the sentence is your smallest unit of composition, and if this smallest unit is ill-shaped and weak, the sum of the units is likely to be ill-shaped and weak as well.

This isn't always true. Faulkner used sentences that were long, shapeless, and rambling, yet nobody would deny the elemental force of his work.

This is also true for Joyce, and for many others. But these were artists, and artists make their own rules. You can, too, if you take yourself seriously as an artist. But if you are like the rest of us, struggling merely with the light of reason and not trying to shape the clay of experience, then you need the conventional tools of communication. You need sentences that are clear, strong, and varied in shape.

18 ✍ Find an Editor

You can look up the mechanics of editing in the back of your dictionary. The famous style manuals of the Government Printing Office, the University of Chicago Press, or the *New York Times* will answer any questions you may have on form, footnotes, references, abbreviations, compound words, etc. What you don't find between the covers of a book is an editor—somebody who can tell you, "This is confusing, this is rambling, this is pedantic."

It is fairly easy to find somebody who is good on commas, can straighten out your sentences, put in the right headings and subheadings, watch out for consistency, and prepare your copy for the typist and the printer. These are the basic and important editing services that take a lot of the drudgery out of your writing chores. In a pinch you can do them yourself. But what you cannot do is function as your own critic without frustrating yourself to the point where it becomes impossible for you to continue writing. Sooner or later, even if you are a genius, you will need a critic—an editor.

Being an editor/critic is very difficult. It takes understanding, decisiveness, a lot of courage, and a lot of tact. It takes someone whom the writer can respect but need not fear; someone who can flatter you without fawning, encourage you with full awareness of the forces he sets in motion, and squelch you where you need to be squelched, but without rancor; someone who can tell you that you are being pedantic and get away with it.

Handholding, fostering, pruning, snipping, squelching, and encouraging have always been the true functions of the editor. The magazine editor is a filter for the articles submitted for publication. Some she will reject outright. Others she may return with an encouraging note requesting future submissions. Still others she may return with specific requests for a rewrite. Some articles she may accept with just some light editing by an assistant. Some may need no work at all, while others require major rewrites on which she or an assistant will work closely with the writer.

All editors function similarly in funneling the writers' work to publication. They are funnels, critics, and perhaps ultimately buyers for the kind of merchandise their customers want.

In a writer's utopia, where there are no editors and no critics and everything gets published, the writers would quickly either become neurotic and stop writing or seek another medium of expression, one that would refuse them uncritical acceptance. Uncritical acceptance is, in fact, no response at all, and no human being can exist for long without some kind of response from his environment, be it good or bad, threatening or benign. All writing is meant to stimulate a response, and without a response it becomes mechanical, lifeless.

The function of the editor is to provide the critical response. As a "buyer" he guides you to what to write. The proposal editor, for example, will be very specific about the kind of input he expects from you. Your employer, asking you for a trip report, is equally specific. And the magazine editor who returns your manuscript with a printed rejection slip tells you clearly that she does not want to buy.

The careful editor will tell you where your presentation is weak and where it needs pruning, clarification, and condensation. He'll ask questions like "What does this mean?" "Does this mean what it says?" or "Who he?" as the late Harold Ross of *The New Yorker* queried his writers about any new character who seemed to be coming out of the woodwork. Your editor will cool you when you're overcome by your own cleverness, and urge you on when you become too timid. He will be your sounding board and your safety valve so that you can let yourself go without fear of making an ass of yourself.

Freeing you from self-consciousness is one of the most important functions of the editor. It's a great feeling for a writer to know that somebody is there to catch your mixed metaphors and dangling clauses, somebody who can keep you honest in your hyperboles and tone down your rich beautiful prose. Overwriting can be a joy in action, one you can indulge yourself in when you know that you have a capable editor who'll rein you in eventually. An editor can easily handle an excess of words—cutting and pruning is the most enjoyable part of the job—but there isn't anything he or she can do with starved, underwritten prose.

It's not easy to find an editor you can trust and respect, but it's worth much effort to find one. Ideally, the editor should know as much about the subject as the writer. But this isn't always possible, nor is it absolutely necessary. Few areas of human knowledge are so abstruse that they are impenetrable to an intelligent person who makes a conscientious effort to understand. Your editor may have to accept your premises, your proof, and your conclusions on faith, but she'll still be able to point out to you where you are obfuscating, begging questions, and fudging answers. She can point out where you need summaries and interpretive paragraphs. And she can make you glow with pride and joy by a simple word of honest praise.

Writing is such a lonely job, even occasional writing. You need all the help you can get. Get an editor.

19 ✍ Stay in the Background

All great portraits are self-portraits. When Flaubert was asked how he, as a man, could think himself so totally into the character of his heroine, Madame Bovary, he replied, "I *am* Emma Bovary." The Saskias, Mona Lisas, Spanish Infantas, and Majas who gaze at us from their museum frames across the centuries touch us not because of what the painter tells us about them but because of what he tells us about himself. The experience of art is that of discovery, discovery of an emotional, spiritual, or intellectual kinship with the artist—but discovery through indirect means because the artist remains in the background, working on us through an objective medium.

Thomas Mann once had one of his characters grumble that he, as a writer, couldn't stand the springtime and all it entailed, preferring to insulate himself against the intrusion of spring by going to a café. Writers, according to Mann, need distance, isolation, objectivity, noninvolvement— insulation if you wish. They need the protection of the coffee house when all around them life is renewing itself, bursting with vigor and thrusting itself on them. The artist is denied participation. He must be aloof.

The reason I am stressing the point here, at the conclusion of my DOs, is my fear of being misunderstood. I have talked at length about point of view, having something unique to say, using personal pronouns, etc. All this does not mean that you should ever push yourself into the foreground, inject your own feelings and opinions at the expense of the objective thing you are writing about.

Inexperienced writers tend to confuse point of view and perspective with having opinions and personal reactions. Writers must have both, but good writers will be careful not to let their opinions and reactions intrude on the subject itself. To do so is brash and ineffectual. It is an immodest attempt to impose yourself on your reader, and nobody likes to be imposed upon.

We may all have known the emotion of a calm evening at the beach when we were glancing out over the ocean into the setting sun. We may be tempted to describe the experience in terms of sense reactions and thought stimuli: our thrills, sense of awe, thoughts of eternity, etc. Here is how Matthew Arnold did it:

> The sea is calm tonight.
> The tide is full, the moon lies fair
> Upon the straits:—on the French coast the light
> Gleams and is gone; the cliffs of England stand
> Glimmering and vast, out in the tranquil bay.
> Come to the window, sweet is the night air.

He evokes an emotion by referring to specific things—sea, tide, moon, light, air. Without ever mentioning himself, he lets us know the texture of his mind.

There may be times when your own subjective reactions and sensations are part of the substance of your report. A test pilot pulling out of a power dive may legitimately describe the effect of gravity on his own clear-headedness. But as a rule, personalization tends to distract the reader from your objective—which is to inform, to influence, to convert.

Part Two

DON'Ts

20 ✍ Surprise Endings

Surprise endings may have a place in literature and storytelling, but they have no place in everyday, ordinary communications. By surprise endings I mean any construction—in a paragraph, a letter, or a report—where the conclusion is deferred until the end. (See "Where to Begin," in Chapter 12, Part One.) The essay writer may not necessarily know what his conclusions will be until he has debated the issue from all angles, clarifying his thoughts through writing. Similarly, the short-story writer may spin her tale toward an unexpected end. But in ordinary, straightforward communications, surprise endings are the most annoying cause of boredom, irritation, and inability to understand. The practice of saving conclusions for the end is, nevertheless, among the most common of all writing faults.

One reason writers use surprise endings is the mistaken belief that they'll achieve greater impact by doing so. One famous and otherwise admirable writer's guide states that "the last part of your paper should be the most important, meaningful, intense, or interesting—it should emphasize the point or points that you want most to impress upon the reader." This is the sort of thing we learned at school and that we have to unlearn before we can become even moderately interesting writers. We have to unlearn it because it puts the emphasis where it doesn't belong. It makes us concentrate on the end when we should be concerned about carrying the reader through the beginning, not to mention the middle. It makes writers hold up the meat course until after dessert and coffee out of fear of having nothing left with which to make an impression. If you've carried your reader with you to the end, you have little to worry about: you've won the battle. If you merely lure him on, letting him chafe and stew, skipping the middle parts to peek at the conclusion, then you've lost at least part of his good will, no matter how admirable your conclusion may be.

Another reason why some writers like surprise endings is that they're trained to think analytically and may feel that they must reproduce the analytical process in their writing. Thus they lay an elaborate foundation of premises on which they build step by step until they reach their conclusion. Eureka! Here it is, the nugget of truth after five thousand words of painful exposition. If your truth is worth stating, come out with it early and take your chances on letting your reader follow you as you present your reasoning.

This misplaced scrupulousness of presenting reasons first and deferring conclusions is especially prevalent among scientists and engineers trained in meticulous work habits. Paragraph after paragraph they'll start out with the premises and end with the conclusions, straining the reader's attention and forcing him continually to guess where they are heading and what they are trying to say. But administrators and bureaucrats share the fault, too. They don't come out and tell you that something has been cancelled or something new is being tried. Instead they present a tortuous exposition of the situation, giving all kinds of reasons and excuses before they hit you with the news.

Many writers instinctively prefer the surprise ending because of their orderly habits of chronological accounting. The passion for sequence is the enemy of clarity. Chronological sequence is usually immaterial in a trip, travel, or test report. Don't bore your readers with meaningless detail about the mechanics of the trip or test on which you are reporting. If the details are necessary, leave them to the body, end, or appendix of the report. Summarize them if you can, but don't put them like a Chinese wall before your readers. Lead them through the gate by giving them the most interesting part first. The most interesting part is, by definition, the part they want to know about. Don't worry about losing their interest by firing your biggest salvo first. Once you've got the most important part of your message across to your readers, they'll follow you further. At a minimum, if they are only mildly interested, they'll pick and choose from the rest of your report. At least you won't have annoyed, lost, or befuddled them. Readers are rare and precious. Treat them well.

21 ✍ Mixed Constructions

Mixed constructions—also called nonparallel or shifted constructions—
are among the most common faults that block understanding. Our minds
are trained to expect parallel constructions. When our expectations are
disappointed, we tend to become confused. It's like finding oranges, apples,
and bananas all growing from the same tree. Wondrous but startling.

Nonparallel constructions present a confusing mix of subjects and
objects, nouns and verbs, adjectives and clauses, active and passive voice,
phrases and adverbs, and other monsters shown below. Where we expect
a noun, we are confronted by a phrase; where we expect the subject to
continue, we find ourselves shifted to another. We object not only because
it is grammatically wrong but also because it makes the meaning hard
to grasp.

Mixed (nonparallel) constructions appear mainly in lists. In ordinary
sentences, most writers avoid this fault; but many writers become careless
when they give lists that are not just parts of a continuous sentence.

Examples

Wrong	Right
A car serves two purposes:	A car serves two purposes. You need it for
1. You can take your girl for a ride.	
2. Transportation.	1. taking your girl for a ride.
	2. transportation.
The new model has many advantages:	
greater speed	greater speed
more economical	better economy
has safety features	more safety features
gives more leg room	more leg room
lower purchase price	lower purchase price

To start car:

a. Insert ignition key.	a. Insert ignition key.
b. Car should be in neutral.	b. Put car in neutral.
c. Gas pedal should be held to floor for two seconds.	c. Press gas pedal to floor for two seconds.
d. Turning the key will now start the motor.	d. Turn key to start motor.

The car has the following features:

1. Accelerates from a cold start to 60 mph in 9 seconds.	1. Acceleration from a cold start to 60 mph in 9 seconds.
2. Pushbutton gear selection.	2. Pushbutton gear selection.
3. The engine is absolutely noiseless.	3. Absolutely noiseless engine.

Military commands:

Attention!—commands soldiers to stand at attention.	Attention!—commands soldiers to stand at attention.
At ease!—soldiers may now relax in place.	At ease!—releases soldiers from "attention."

In our problem:

N is the multiplicand.	N is the multiplicand.
n is the multiplier.	n is the multiplier.
s if n is a fraction, then s is the quotient.	s is the quotient if n is a fraction.

But mixed constructions also crop up in ordinary sentences (correct forms in parentheses):

Studying the subject, understanding the difficulties, and to realize (realizing) how much I had to learn discouraged me.

The house is bright, comfortably furnished, and you'll feel right at home in it. (The house is bright and comfortably furnished, and makes you feel right at home.)

The reader believes she is told one thing until you realize you are told something else. (. . . until she realizes that she is told something else.)

Washington is famous for its broad avenues, for its fine monuments, and because it is the seat of government. (. . . and for being the seat of government.)

The new chief engineer has an M.S. from MIT, 15 years experience and lives in Santa Barbara. (. . . has an M.S. . . . and 15 years experience. He lives in Santa Barbara.)

The set is distinguished by its attractiveness, compactness, it has no protruding parts, and costs less than others. (The set is attractive and compact, has no protruding parts, and costs less than others.)

The toaster is 10 inches long, 6 inches in width, and has a height of 5 inches. (. . . is 10 inches long, 6 inches wide, and 5 inches high.)

Among the reasons men choose a career in the foreign service are social advantages they hope to enjoy, they expect to lead adventurous lives, training for a useful position, because of uncertainty about their future, and in order to get an education. (Reasons men choose a career in the foreign service are expectations of social advantages and an adventurous life, the prospect of receiving training for a useful position, uncertainty about their future, and the desire to get an education.)

Young men enter West Point for the prestige of a military career, they want financial security, out of genuine patriotism, the fulfillment of a lifelong ambition, and because they get a free education. (Young men enter West Point for the prestige of a military career, financial security, genuine patriotism, the fulfillment of a lifelong ambition, and a free education.)

22 ✍ Self-Serving Words

Words are self-serving when they claim approval without submitting proof. They are words that try to preempt independent judgment, words that assign values without show of evidence. Self-serving words are adjectives like good, bad, excellent, magnificent, marvelous, select, elite, outstanding, maximum, minimum, unprecedented, unrivaled, optimum, favored, satisfied, etc. These words are tolerable and possibly unavoidable in conversation and disinterested description; they should be used sparingly if at all in promotional material. The difference is that all promotional material is self-serving by nature and is accepted as such, engendering in readers an automatic willingness to discount and disbelieve your message as propaganda. They know you are going to woo them, and possibly snow them. If they are predisposed to be wooed, they will be tolerant toward your superlatives. But if they are skeptical, your self-serving prose will not convince them and may make them angry and hostile. They'll consider your adjectives empty bragging, and you can't blame them. (See Chapter 44, "How to Brag," for a better alternative to self-serving adjectives.)

23 ✍ Passive Voice

An example of the passive voice is "The XYZ phenomenon *was investigated.*" This pattern of writing seems peculiarly seductive. Once writers acquire the habit of writing in the passive voice, they use it over and over, frequently to the point of eliminating the strong active voice altogether.

There are two valid reasons and some invalid ones for using the passive voice. Valid reasons are emphasis and deliberate obfuscation. Invalid reasons include a false sense of objectivity; misplaced scrupulousness; pretentiousness; and uncertainty.

First, the legitimate uses. You may have to use the passive voice to emphasize a point:

> Button A is pushed first, before any of the others.
>
> This rule must be obeyed: the others are optional.

In both these cases, placing the object at the head of the sentence gives it an emphasis that would be lost with an active-voice construction.

When you don't want to be exact, you may use the passive voice:

> These funds may be used only in an emergency.
>
> The computer memory may be accessed only when . . .

What is missing in both these examples is a specification of *who* may use the funds and *what* or *who* may access the computer memory. The omitted part may be implicit, but it may also be due to deliberate vagueness: obfuscation or uncertainty. For example, Article I, paragraph 9, 2, of our Constitution states that "the right of *habeas corpus* shall not be suspended, unless when in cases of rebellion or invasion the public safety may require it." It is moot whether this wording was the result of deliberate vagueness or simply irresolution on the part of the drafters of the Constitution, but failure to state who had the right to suspend *habeas corpus* did create trouble when President Lincoln invoked the clause during the Civil War. Who did have the right? The President, as Lincoln assumed? Or the Supreme Court? Or the legislature? The vagueness of the wording, deliberate or accidental, provided leeway for interpretation—and for litigation.

Among the illegitimate reasons for using the passive voice, a false quest for objectivity stands out. A statement does not gain in stature by being made in the passive voice. Similarly, a false sense of scrupulousness may induce some writers to use the passive voice. They may claim legitimately that abstractions like government, program, state, etc. can't do anything by themselves; but they'll extend this scrupulousness to machines, hesitating to state that machines do perform real actions. Such writers are technically correct to avoid claiming material properties for something abstract, but their correctness is pedantic and unimportant—even self-defeating—from the point of view of style.

The passive voice may give a simple statement an air of importance it would not otherwise have. "This exit is to be used only in an emergency" sounds grander than the simple "emergency exit"; and "Two alternative approaches were considered" seems to be more dignified than "We considered two alternative approaches." Needless to say, these are false appearances, symptoms of pretentiousness.

Laziness is a major reason for using the passive voice. This is especially true in technical writing, where a passive construction may save the writer the trouble of finding out what actually happens. "The gas and air mixture is compressed and ignited" is a lazy and foreshortened way of stating that the piston compresses the gas and air mixture inside the cylinder and that the spark from the spark plug then ignites the compressed mixture. The short version is permissible when we are dealing with well-known phenomena, but it becomes evasion when the writer tries to explain a new process. He may not be quite sure about the interaction of the parts of a machine or a system. Using the passive voice spares him the labor of achieving certainty and the risk of making a guess.

It is easy to illustrate this point, but difficult to find examples that make sense to the general reader. "The tangent models are initialized to some operating point and a set of node voltages are determined." "Groups of functions were pulled together under each of the principal directors reporting to the division president where they were clearly interrelated." "The instruction can be interrupted during the course of its execution, and can then be resumed without producing an erroneous result." "An analogy can be drawn with a flagpole." All four examples are from published material. They suffer from other structural weaknesses, too, but the passive voice compounds the difficulties.

Aside from the functional reasons for avoiding the passive voice, the overriding ones for me are its monotony and inelegance. The evils of monotony are self-evident, but for the nonprofessional writer the virtue of "mere elegance" is perhaps harder to accept. It shouldn't be. Actually it is the mathematician and scientist who habitually speak of and strive for "elegance," but the writer/editor need not apologize for his efforts to achieve it. Elegance is more than ornamental. It denotes economy and efficiency as much as grace. Elegance is style. And style is of the essence.

24 ✍ *Vitiated Verbs*

A particularly undesirable by-product of the passive voice is the use of vitiated, or debased, verbs. A vitiated verb is one that has been turned into a noun but continues to take the place of the verb by appearing in combination with an auxiliary or some other "weak" verb. Examples:

Vitiated	Active/Strong
An indication of . . . is provided by . . .	The . . . indicates that . . .
Repayment will be made . . .	We will repay . . .
Consideration is given to . . .	We are considering . . .
Make an adjustment of . . .	Adjust . . .
An evaluation has been made . . .	We have evaluated . . .
The writer has an appreciation of . . .	We appreciate/like . . .
An inclination is shown by . . .	. . . inclines
The operation was performed . . .	The doctor operated . . .
Attribution of the remarks was made to . . .	He attributed the remarks to . . .
An investigation has been undertaken of . . .	We have investigated/studied . . .
A positive rating was arrived at by . . .	We rated . . . positive because . . .
An analysis has been made of . . .	We have analyzed . . .
A report has been released by . . .	XYZ has reported that . . .
Emphasis should be placed on . . .	. . . should be emphasized
An improvement has been made in . . .	. . . has been improved

Verbs are the muscles and sinews of language. They move your sentences forward and make your words flow. Each time you change a verb into a noun you slow your cadence and lower the pressure. You break your stride when you vitiate verbs.

25  Too Many Prepositions

Excessive use of prepositions (words like *of, in, by, on, out, to, under, through*) is still another by-product of the passive voice and vitiated verbs. These prepositions create clutter and slack. They force the reader to read more laboriously than he would read something written in the active voice with pure instead of vitiated verbs.

> The establishment *of* an independent authority *for* the coordination *of* a nationwide fight *against* crime, and provision *of* generous financial support *for* properly reorganized state and local systems was urged *by* a panel *of* national business leaders.

This sentence, written in the passive voice, contains eight prepositions. Rewritten in the active voice and without vitiated verbs, the sentence contains only three prepositions:

> A panel *of* national business leaders has urged that an independent authority be established to coordinate a nationwide fight *against* crime and provide generous financial support *for* properly reorganized state and local systems.

Which is better?

According to Webster's Dictionary, a preposition is "a word generally with some meaning of position, direction, time, or other abstract relation used to connect a noun or pronoun . . . with some other word." This dictionary definition throws some light on the difficulties too many prepositions can create. They force the reader to establish and remember abstract relationships. If you throw too many at him in one sentence, you are apt to confuse him. As a rule of thumb, four prepositions per sentence should be enough, especially for an essentially simple, declarative sentence like the above example. But remember that the prepositions are only the by-product. It's the communicative attitude that counts. If you use too many prepositions, it means that you're not facing the reader.

26 ✍️ *Redundancies*

If you describe an object as red in color and round in shape, you're really nailing it down, taking no chance on being misunderstood. But you're also betraying insecurity and will bore your reader to tears. This kind of writing lacks crispness. It's limp.

The following list gives examples of redundancies that should be avoided. The words in parentheses are the portion of the phrase that can (and should) be omitted without risk of weakening it or changing its meaning.

Because (of the fact that)
The maximum (possible) amount
A range (all the way) from
A (time) interval or period
An (innumerable) number of
(Final) climax
(Capping) the climax
Assemble (together)
Connect (together)
Add (together)
Connect (up)
Fuse (together)
Square (in shape)
Few (in number)
Big (in size)
Adequate (enough)
(Entirely) completed
Atop (of)
Inside (of)

The modern man (of today)
(Every) now and then
Total effect of (all) this
Mutual advantage (of both)
(Surrounding) circumstances
Endorse (on the back)
They are (both) alike
Favorable condition for warping
   (to occur)
Necessary (requisite)
(True) facts
(Successful) achievements
Recoil (back)
Repeat (again)
Return (back)
Each (and every)
Thus (as a result)
Continue (on)
Termed (as)

All (of)
(And) moreover
This (same) program
Equally (as) willing
The same (identical) meaning
Throughout (the whole of)
Bisect (into two parts)
Halved (in two parts)
(Most) unique
Bald (-headed) man

Blue (in color)
(Still) persists
Might (possibly)
(As) yet
(But) nevertheless
The pregnant Chinese (woman)
(As to) whether
2 p.m. (in the afternoon)
(New) beginners

27 ✍ Clutter and Fence Sitting

Vague, imprecise, and roundabout expressions lack crispness. In conversation, you can get away with imprecision because you can emphasize and reinforce your statements by intonation and gestures; and you can supply additional information if necessary. In writing, vagueness and imprecision—at worst annoying in conversation—may become frustrating to the reader looking for information.

State exact quantities and use exact terminology wherever possible. For example, don't say *some* improvement when you can say *a 30 percent* improvement; a *considerable* amount when you can say *a million dollars; several* questions remain to be answered for *three* questions remain to be answered. Similarly it is better to *bolt, screw, snap, rivet,* or *strap* one thing to another than to *attach* it; and it is best to supply exact terminology for the two things attached.

There is a long list of fence-sitting expressions that the forceful writer will avoid. To hedge your bets in the stock market is one thing, to do it in writing is quite another. To the hedging writer, there are always "possibilities that seem to suggest," "tentative" conclusions, "preliminary" observations, "envisioned" solutions, and "general rules, certainly not applicable in all situations." What is most objectionable about such phrasing is the writer's attitude. The writer of the following memorandum (actually written and submitted) must have a mind as crisp as a wet noodle.

> As a general rule, and certainly not applicable in all situations, the briefing memoranda forwarded to the secretary have been loaded with an excessive amount of verbiage. In the future, the briefing memoranda should highlight the issue, set forth alternative courses of action or approaches to resolve the issue, and finally, a recommendation regarding the action to be taken by the secretary should be made with reasons therefor. It is envisioned that this sort of writing will not require more than a page and a half to two pages at the most. Additional supporting data, information, comments, and supporting documentation may be included beneath the writing referred to above, as deemed necessary.
>
> The secretary does not, in any way, intend that the free flow of information to him be restricted or limited. However, he does desire that the central issue be highlighted and acted upon in the manner set forth in this memorandum.

A reasonable translation of the memorandum would read:

> Briefing memoranda to the secretary are often too long. They should simply highlight the issue, present alternatives, and make reasoned recommendations. This should require not more than a page and a half. Supporting data can be appended as necessary.
>
> The secretary does not want less information; he wants it to be better presented.

The point of the rewrite isn't just that it's shorter—which it is by more than half; the real improvement is that it is clearer, and more to the point. It is simpler, much more direct, and much warmer. Notice particularly all the unnecessary words left out in the rewrite. Redundancy is legitimate when you want to underscore an important point by repeating a statement in reworded form. However, when you do this, make sure that the reworded statement is properly introduced and identified as a restatement; that is, make sure that you remove all doubt from the reader's mind about whether you are introducing a new thought or repeating one previously stated. This is what I did in the preceding sentence where I introduced the restatement of my thought by the phrase "that is." Other phrases commonly used for this purpose are "i.e." (Latin for *id est*, "that is"), "in other words," or "stated in another way." But this stylistic device should be used sparingly. The redundancies in the example memo are counterproductive. Instead of reinforcing, they confuse. What is the meaning of "additional supporting data, information, comments, and supporting documentation"? Do you lose anything by lumping them all under "supporting data"? Doesn't the longer version actually force you into a useless mental scan of alternative interpretations? What is the use of all the backing and filling at the beginning of the memorandum? Once you analyze it, you'll find it to be nothing but garbage, dressed up to give the appearance of meaning it doesn't have.

Beware also of bureaucratic phrases like "with reference to," "on behalf of," "regarding," etc. Official, formal writing is frequently larded with these usually meaningless phrases. We are so used to seeing them that our writing often doesn't look right to us without them. It may be tedious at first to scrutinize each of these expressions for its meaning to see whether or not it is really needed, but after a while, leaving out the dross of useless phrases will become a habit—and your writing will gain directness and crispness. Given below is a list of bureaucratic phrases to watch out for and to eliminate whenever possible.

Bureaucratic Phrases and Alternatives

Bureaucratic	Direct
by means of	by
in the event of	if
along the lines of	like, as
with the result that / designed so that	so that
in order to / with a view toward / for the purpose of	to
for the reason that / on the grounds that / on the basis of	because, since
in connection with / in relation to, with regard to, with respect to, in the matter of	about

In the same league as the bureaucratic phrases are indirect expressions like "there are" and "it is." Most of the time you can avoid these expressions by starting your sentence with the noun or pronoun that is being circumvented, or with an imperative. For example, "it is our understanding that" can be shortened (and strengthened) to "we understand"; "there are three questions" to "three questions"; "it should be noted that" to "note that." In the last case, even the "note that" may be superfluous. The thing to be noted is frequently more noticeable when it stands without an introduction. Then there are the polite little stereotypes that serve absolutely no purpose other than to slow down and confuse your reader. In the following sentences, the words in parentheses are the stereotypes that should be left out.

(This is to inform you that) Mr. Broadbeam will call on you at your office (as) soon (as possible).

(We are pleased to direct your attention to) paragraph 8 (which) indicates that . . .

Please (feel free to) write (to this office) if you (find yourself in) need (of) additional details.

(Data obtained during) flight tests indicate that . . .

It may be argued that in all these examples it would take only a fraction of a second to read the extra words, and that leaving them in makes the phrasing more courteous and more exact. I'd gladly go along with this if the premise were correct. But it is not correct. I'd go along even if the extra words were simply harmless, neither adding to nor subtracting from the whole. But they do subtract. They are clutter words that divert attention and impede understanding. They represent separate ideas the reader must absorb before he gets to the main idea. It may not take him very long to do so, but the effect is cumulative. Clutter words brake reading speed and reduce impact. One of the worst clutter words is the innocuous definite article "the." Yet it is difficult to formulate a rule on when to use and when not to use the definite article. I once edited the manuscript of an author who was a recent immigrant from Poland. Polish seems to possess no definite article, and my author had left it out throughout his paper (written in English). The experience gave me an appreciation of the value of the humble word "the." Nevertheless, it's easy to use it to excess, slowing down your reader. Let your ear be your guide and remember that modern usage favors a more elliptical style where the definite article is implied rather than stated.

28 ✍ *Pompous Words*

Like bureaucratic phrases and indirect expressions, pompous words are stereotypes that make writing stiff and lifeless. Most authorities agree that it is better to use short, simple words of Anglo-Saxon origin than their longer equivalents with Latin roots. The short and simple words are usually strong and direct, whereas the Latinate ones are often tainted with formality and stiffness. They tend to sound pompous. Examine the following words carefully before you use them:

prior to (before)	remunerate/compensate (pay)
initiate (start)	transmit (send)
terminate (end)	personnel (people)
utilize (use)	subsequent (next)

The shorter word given in parentheses is almost always better.

The pressure for using the pompous words is admittedly strong. They do seem to sound grander and to convey an air of importance that the simple words lack. But you should resist the temptation to use them if possible. The simple word will almost always convey exactly the same meaning as the grander one and will help you become a little more relaxed in your attitude as a communicator. People who use pompous words and phrases begin to stiffen inwardly, too. They no longer expect anything; they anticipate. They don't use "same" if "identical" is available at the same price. Sometimes they even use both. They know only individuals, not persons, and personnel instead of people. It takes a little time to get used to the simpler words, but it's worth the trouble.

Shakespeare, even though he was no slouch himself at using long and even made-up words, had one of his characters in one of his earliest plays speak out against the artificiality and sterility of this kind of pompous language, pleading for "honest yeas and russet nays." Using big words is an old ploy, and one to watch out for.

Who or Whom

And while we're on the subject of pompous words, we might heed the opinion of the late Kyle Crichton, associate editor of the old *Collier's* magazine. "The most loathsome word (to me at least) in the English language is WHOM," writes Crichton. "You can always tell a half-educated buffoon by the care he takes in working the word in. When he starts it, I know I am faced with a pompous illiterate who is not going to have me long as company." Having detected misplaced WHOMs in the prose of reputable and enjoyable writers, including "Dear Abby," I don't go quite so far as Mr. Crichton, but I do advise being cautious in putting the "m" on "who." Foreigners brought up in strange tongues that clearly distinguish the nominative case from the dative and accusative never seem to have any trouble in differentiating between "who" and "whom," but those whose native tongue is English apparently have difficulty. People who are self-confident about their education will drop the "m" without hesitation whenever they are in doubt and even be proud of the nice colloquial touch they provide with an ungrammatical but acceptable "who." They do far better than the gentleman quoted by George Ade who asked, "Whom are you?"—for he had been to night school.

And/Or

Not nearly so bad but still objectionable when misused is the ubiquitous "and/or." U.S. Congresswoman Shirley Chisholm once said that she "didn't care if a person was black and/or white," and I haven't ceased to wonder if she meant black, speckled, or white. The distinction between "and" and "or" is usually clear-cut or trivial, and using "and/or" for one or the other is the result of either sloppy habit or mental laziness. "And/or" is rarely justified, and in the few cases where it is, it's better to use a few extra words and spell out the difference. Logically "and/or" is justified only when there is both a choice of two alternatives and the possibility of the two alternatives occurring together. "The offense is punishable by one year's imprisonment and/or a $1000 fine" means you can get one or the other or both. In "dancing and/or playing music is forbidden on Sundays," the phrase is meaningless and should be replaced by "or." "Or" is the enemy of "and," which permits of no choice. In most cases you either have a choice or you don't. It is either A *or* B, or A *and* B. If it is truly A *and/or* B, it is generally best to write "A or B or both."

Such That

"Such that" is still another phrase that is frequently misused. It is correct only when the preceding noun could be repeated after "such" without loss of meaning:

> The effect is *such* (an effect) *that* . . .
> When the result is *such* (a result) *that* . . .

In these examples the *such* is used correctly. The antecedent (preceding) noun can be repeated without loss of meaning. This could not be done in the following examples, where *such* is misused:

> We have achieved a design such that (*so that*) the system can operate without human intervention.
> The vectors are computed such that (*so that*) convergence occurs. . . .

The use of the phrase is wrong in both examples: "so that" is the only correct form. You cannot possibly repeat the antecedent noun after "such."

Buzz Words

To complete this discussion a few words should be said about "buzz words"—words that automatically set off buzzers. They are the stimuli in the stimulus-response system of the writer-reader relationship. As reported by *Newsweek* magazine some years ago, a U.S. Public Health Service official by the name of Philip Broughton even invented a Systematic Buzz Phrase Projector consisting of 30 carefully chosen buzz words that he arranged in three columns:

Column 1	*Column 2*	*Column 3*
0. integrated	0. management	0. options
1. total	1. organizational	1. flexibility
2. systematized	2. monitored	2. capability
3. parallel	3. reciprocal	3. mobility
4. functional	4. digital	4. programming
5. responsive	5. logistical	5. concept
6. optional	6. transitional	6. time-phase
7. synchronized	7. incremental	7. projection
8. compatible	8. third-generation	8. hardware
9. balanced	9. policy	9. contingency

Any combination of three numbers will result in a knowledgeable-sounding buzz phrase. For example, 685 comes to "optional third-generation concept" and 521 to "responsive monitored flexibility." Either phrase will reflect credit on a report writer, investing him with a degree of authority no one will ever question.

Clichés

Foreigners learning a new language usually fall in love with clichés. To their virgin ears, the trite phrases we call clichés have all the charm and novelty that caused them originally to become overused and hackneyed. "Dead as a dodo" and "old as the hills," once felicitous expressions, have become obnoxious only because of mindless repetition. Fortunately, this is the type of cliché that writers can easily be warned against and editors can easily cope with. The major trouble is that writers using such clichés reveal themselves as unskilled and inexperienced. But the damage itself can be repaired. Less reparable is the damage inflicted by borderline, unsuspected, and conceptual clichés. "Relate," "lifestyle," "structured," "dialogue," "parenting," "bottomline," and "meaningful" are examples of clichés that set my teeth on edge because we have no defenses against them. What can you do with people who think it's nice to be "creative" and apply the term to somebody who does number painting? How do you cope with people who "do research" when they consult the encyclopedia? How do you deal with writers who have no hesitation about "the establishment," "involvement," and "providing success experiences" to "underachievers"? Or, on the other hand, what about those who "tell it like it is" and "get down to the nitty gritty"? What do we do about "charisma" when this somewhat mystic quality is attributed to a nice set of teeth or wavy hair? How do we deal with Oedipus and inferiority "complexes," "sibling rivalries," "identity crises," and the "socially and culturally deprived"? The trouble with all these words and phrases is that they have become debased by overuse and have lost their intended meaning; they are stereotypes.

Words become debased when writers use them mechanically without thinking about their original meaning, when they use them like shorthand notation where a simple word substitutes for something that is complex and intricate. In a sense, this is the function of words—but only to a point. The point is reached when the conceptual freight the word once carried becomes so eroded that it can be used indiscriminately in almost any situation. I once counted the word "image" 36 times during two minutes of a PR man's lecture. Now, admittedly, image is a good word and image-building is what PR people do. When you talk about public relations, the word "image" is hard to avoid. Yet it should be possible. One could talk about a company's identity or of the public's conception of the company; the idea the company conveys, the picture of itself it creates, the impression it wants to make, or the misconceptions some people have of it; the company's impact on the public's imagination, the company's role, or its specific aura; the fear or love the company generates, its known benevolence, its interest in public service, or its callousness to public welfare. It can all be summed up in the one word: image. But the one word just isn't good enough any more. It is sheer laziness to use this one word that fits all occasions when a little thought and knowledge will lead you to phrases that are specific and tangible.

"Ecology" is another fad word. How many people are even able to define what it really means: that it comes from the Greek word *oikos*, meaning house, and stands for the science of housekeeping, applied to the environment? No one can be faulted for being "concerned with the ecology," but how much more interesting it is to talk about just one specific case of environmental death or decay than to resort to the safe generality of "ecology."

My own remedy when words like "lifestyle" seem to just flow into the typewriter is to pause and think about what I really have in mind: sexual license? reluctance to bathe? compulsive work habits? We really don't have to use the easy word if we're willing to give a little thought to what, specifically, we want to say. More difficult to avoid is the word "creative." It is so pleasant to refer to one's child's (or one's own) "creative" personality to excuse shortcomings in some other area where we (or the child) don't function as well. But we can avoid the cliché by being more specific. We may say the child is ruminative, imaginative, sensitive, oversensitive, shy, self-absorbed, or brooding. We may say that he or she has difficulty making friends and compensates for it by making up stories peopled with imagined friends; or that he or she likes to paint, model clay, make paper dolls, or do needlework. We don't have to say that someone is creative. The term is so broad it's meaningless. We can (and must) apply it to the genius of Michelangelo; but we shouldn't use it to describe the obscure copywriter—no matter how talented—who doesn't change our vision or thinking. For that is what "creative" really means: the ability to recreate our world so that we'll look at it with new eyes. It's something that only the geniuses have done, and the word should remain reserved for them. Perhaps the word should be abandoned altogether, at least temporarily.

And that's what we should do with all the clichés: abandon them, give them a rest, let them lie fallow for a while. After a rest, to a new generation they may again appear fresh and "meaningful."

29 ✍ Confusing the Fruit with the Tree

You erect a major block to understanding when you put the apple on the same level of description as the apple tree. From infancy on, our intellectual development consists of little more than assimilating larger and larger classes of things. By learning to associate the specific with the general, we achieve the widening of our perspective that marks our intellectual growth. Classifying thus becomes an instinctive part of the learning process.

When we impart information—when we write or teach—we reverse this part of the learning process. We begin by establishing classes and continue by developing subclasses for each of the classes. That is, we begin by establishing the class "tree," dividing this class into subclasses (coniferous trees, leaf trees), finally arriving at fruit trees, and eventually at the fruit itself. We develop a hierarchy in which the top rank is the most general class, the superset, and each lower rank represents a subset of the higher-ranking set. We start with a generalization and proceed to increasingly specific levels of detail.

As pointed out in Chapter 13 ("Organize—Then Outline"), organizing material is a most difficult task that requires a thorough understanding of the thing described. Lack of understanding will show up in faulty organization. It will result in a hierarchical structure that simply won't work. For example, in describing the structure of the American government, we would automatically start with the three coordinate branches: executive, legislative, and judicial. Then under the superset "Legislative Branch," we would place two subsets: House and Senate. Someone who didn't know the structure of the American government might be tempted to skip the superset of the legislative branch and substitute House and Senate on the same level as the other two branches, thereby creating four coordinate branches, instead of the three that actually exist. He would have elevated a subordinate level to coordinate level, messing up the established hierarchy. This can, of course, happen in any kind of description, whether it is the American government, an apple tree, or an automobile. It is easy to see how improper subordination can create confusion.

One means of detecting faulty organization is an aesthetic test. A diagram of your organizational structure will give you a quick and unambiguous picture of the "shape" of your report. If the hierarchical pyramid you have developed has too broad a base and too low an apex, you can be almost certain that you have not detected a sufficient number of subclasses in your subject matter. Similarly, if your pyramid is shaped like a stele—long and narrow—then you evidently have too many major and too few minor classes. Either shape denotes faulty coordination and subordination of topics—an organizational error.

Another test of organizational shape is to look at your outline in terms of the number of subordination symbols you use. As a rule of thumb, subordination beyond a fourth-order heading should be regarded with suspicion, and in small- to medium-sized documents even a fourth-order heading may be excessive. On the other hand, if you never go beyond a second-order heading, then something is evidently wrong, too. (Some simple examples of proper and faulty organizational shapes are given in Fig. 29-1.)

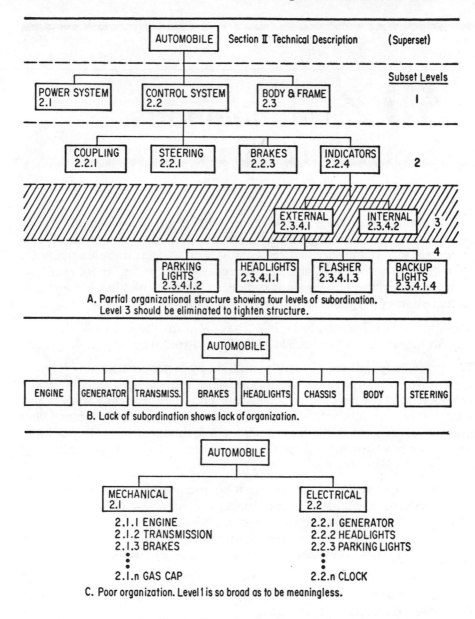

A. Partial organizational structure showing four levels of subordination.
Level 3 should be eliminated to tighten structure.

B. Lack of subordination shows lack of organization.

C. Poor organization. Level 1 is so broad as to be meaningless.

Fig. 29–1. Organizational structures.

30 ✍ *Monotonous Sentence Structure*

The first thing everybody learns about writing is that sentences should be short. Word count or syllable count per sentence is considered one important index of clarity and readability. And there is more than a grain of truth in this. As a rule, short sentences are clearer and more readable than long ones. But writing short sentences is not an end in itself and can do more harm than good if it is made into a principle.

> Jack and Jill went up the hill. They went up the hill to fetch a pail of water. Jack fell down. He broke his crown. Jill came tumbling after.

This is precisely the kind of writing you'll see from people who have learned their lesson about writing only short sentences. They break up every sentence into little declarative statements, endlessly repeating subject and verb. Aside from its sheer tedium, this kind of writing doesn't in any way improve clarity. On the contrary, separating thoughts into distinct units will frequently destroy a "connectedness" without which understanding becomes much harder.

> In the course of human events it sometimes becomes necessary to take certain actions. It may become necessary for one nation to sever the political bonds that tie it to another. In this case, a decent respect to the opinions of mankind requires an explanation. The nation severing its ties must state the reasons for so doing.

Which is clearer? Which is more forceful? Thomas Jefferson's original sweeping sentence or this chopped-up version of it? Or let's rewrite the Gettysburg Address:

> Eighty-seven years ago our forefathers founded a new nation on this continent. The new nation was based on the principle of freedom. It was dedicated to the idea that all men are created equal. Now we are in the midst of a great civil war. The war will decide whether this nation can last, etc.

The parody here is obvious. What is less obvious is that this kind of writing is constantly being perpetrated by people who think they have to write short, choppy, starved little sentences to be understood. To repeat, writing short sentences is not an end in itself.

On the contrary, a succession of short, evenly structured sentences will become so monotonous it will put your reader to sleep. To break monotony, you must vary sentence length and sentence structure (as well as paragraph length and paragraph structure).

Having indicted short sentences as a goal for writing improvement, I must quickly retract any implication that long sentences are necessarily better.

> Having gone up the hill to fetch a pail of water, Jack, accompanied by Jill, fell down and broke his crown whereupon Jill came tumbling after.

This construction is fairly typical of much that is written every day in business, technical, and professional communications. It shows a passion for unnecessary pigeonholing—for subordinate clauses that defeat clarity. The sentence conveys a false sense of logical ordering; its careful sequencing and subordination give it a sheen of pseudo-sophistication that is lacking in the straightforward nursery rhyme. When dealing with a "serious" subject, many writers would find the simpler form almost naive. Again and again they will resort to the complex structure for no better reason than to create an illusion of scrupulousness not demanded by the subject matter.

Scrupulousness—despite its honorable intent—frequently thwarts clarity, readability, and forcefulness. It leads to qualifications; qualifications lead to complications; and complications create confusion. If you must qualify a statement, be careful not to let your sentence structure get away from you.

> Miss Muffet, called "little" because she is presumably a child, which would mean that the appellation "Miss" is to be taken in a playful sense, having sat down on a tuffet, that is, a mound, to eat her curds and whey—a dish popular in the days before milk was sold pasteurized so that it was possible to let it set, thicken, and separate into curds at the bottom and whey at the top—was frightened away by a spider that came along and sat down beside her.

This type of sentence is not at all unusual or infrequent in all types of technical descriptions. The explanations and qualifications may be necessary, but they could easily be given in separate sentences at the end of the two "story" sentences of the nursery rhyme. Combining the two sentences into one dilutes their strength without any gain in sequence or logic.

Long sentences may become troublesome not because they contain too many words but because they contain too many ideas.

> Now, and to an increasing degree as war and Reconstruction recede into the past, the Court's history becomes a history of response to the advance of what was later to be called "the general welfare state."

The first idea in this sentence is position in time: "Now." This idea is immediately qualified by the introduction of a dynamic element related to time: "to an increasing degree as war . . ." This qualification is then further qualified by contrasting the increase in degree with the receding into the past of two eras: "war and Reconstruction." Having digested this fairly complex time relationship, you must now attack the main idea which is again expressed in time-related terms: "response advance . . . later." To understand this sentence your mind has to swing back and forth. You lose the thread if you don't keep continually alert. I would suggest rewriting this sentence as follows:

> As war and Reconstruction recede into the past, the Court reacts with increasing vigor against the advances of what we now call "the general welfare state."

This rewrite simplifies the time relationship; it eliminates the unnecessary concept of "history"; and it substitutes "reacts with increasing vigor" for the weak "response." The meaning of the sentence hasn't changed, but it is now clearer, more forceful, less confusing.

It should be reemphasized that shortening a sentence is no virtue in itself. Some of the best English prose consists of long and sweeping sentences. Examples can be found in Churchill's speeches and in Ecclesiastes, in the writings of the Founders of the Republic and in William Buckley. But most of the time you'll find that these masterful sentences are lists, simple in structure despite their length. Simplicity is not synonymous with conciseness, nor is sweep synonymous with length. If you have the ear, if you have an innate sense of balance and rhythm, then you should at least experiment with longer sentences. If you don't have it, you're better off sticking to the shorter ones. But long or short, try at all times to keep the content simple. And don't strive for too much conciseness.

> The patient left the hospital urinating freely.

In this example, the writer tried to be too concise. He wanted to avoid being long-winded in saying, "When the patient left the hospital, he was able to . . ." In addition to its being right, there is nothing wrong with this looser kind of sentence. Adding just a few necessary words can make all the difference in readability and clarity.

There is almost no limit to what one can say about sentence structure, but these points are important:

1.   Avoid monotony by varying sentence length and structure.
2.   Whenever possible, avoid putting more than one idea into a sentence. It isn't the length so much as the content that makes some sentences hard to digest.
3.   Construct one long sentence rather than two short ones that break up the connectedness of the parts of a thought.

4. Disregard sentence length in lists where all objects are associated with the same subject.
5. Beware of too many qualifying and commenting clauses. When you have more than one dependent clause, it is usually best to start a new sentence.
6. Avoid stating complex time relationships in a sentence that contains other ideas as well.
7. And remember: when in doubt, read it aloud.

You should also watch out for monotonous paragraph construction. The length of paragraphs, too, should be varied for the sake of liveliness and reader interest.

31 ✍ *Cryptic Titles and Captions*

In journalism, headline writing is a highly valued specialty. Newspaper editors know the importance of headlines in arousing interest and of subheads in leading the reader further into the story. Unfortunately, this commonsense practice of using descriptive and interesting headings and subheadings is all too often neglected by nonjournalists.

Chapters, sections, and subsections should all have headings that describe the subject they are treating. This has three advantages: (1) it keeps the writer honest by forcing him to think functionally about his subject instead of just rambling on; (2) it relieves reader anxiety by breaking up long pages of text into manageable modules; and (3) it gives readers needed orientation. Readers can anticipate what they are about to read and set up the proper mental attitude.

The most important function of the heading is to focus the reader's attention. The well-written newspaper headline gives you the whole story in capsule format, or at least presents some sort of conclusion capable of arousing your interest. For example, "Third Man in Kidnap Case Hinted"; "Two UC Regents Clash over Land Dealings with Irvine Co."; "Board's Battle over Use of Stadium for Parade Rally Told." These are three samples picked at random from one page of a newspaper. All three "tell a story."

A similar technique can be used for reports. Whenever possible, avoid the merely categorical heading like "Technical Description," "Management Plan," "Kidnap Case," "Regents Meeting Report," or "Stadium Use for Parade Rally." A lot of reports feature these flat, categorical, nondescriptive, uninteresting titles, usually from a false sense of neutrality and objectivity.

There are times, in manuals for example, when you simply have no choice but to use nondescriptive headings like "Theory of Operation," etc. They may be mandatory if you're writing to a specification, or they may actually be the only ones that fit; but each time you use them you should weigh the question of more descriptive alternatives.

In addition to creating interest for the reader, the informative title can also be a great help to the writer. Most writers have experienced blissful spurts of writing fluently and apparently well, only to stop after a while to ask themselves just what it was they were trying to say. A descriptive title provides direction. It gives the needed focus without which writing easily becomes rambling and discursive.

Subsections and paragraphs should be titled to the extent that the title gives the reader needed orientation. The rule of thumb is that each topic is identified by a title. In some instances this will require titles for each of a series of paragraphs. In others, it may take many untitled paragraphs before a topic is exhausted. Identifying each subject as it is about to be introduced will help you keep your reader with you all the way.

The risk in giving too many subtitles is that you tend to lose smooth transitions and your writing becomes choppy. No firm rule will help you strike the proper balance between too many and too few subtitles. Your own or your editor's judgment will have to be the final arbiter of what's right and what's wrong. But it is important to be aware of the problem of missing and nondescriptive titles and subtitles on the one hand, and of choppiness resulting from too many subtitles on the other.

Even more important than text titles are titles (or captions) for illustrations and tables. One school of thought maintains that these titles should be short, but I strongly disagree with this. A figure or table title should be as long as necessary to make it fully descriptive. Each figure or table should be as self-sufficient and self-explanatory as possible, capable of being understood without reference to the associated text. Frequently this cannot be done with a short title. It is definitely better to be redundant than to leave the reader puzzled over the meaning of a cryptic title.

32 🖎 Colorful Language

Every writer secretly yearns to write rich, colorful prose, but most professional writers have enough sense to restrain themselves most of the time. It's like what the late Beardsley Ruml once said about exercising. "Whenever I feel the urge," he said, "I simply sit down and wait for it to go away." (Ruml is the man who invented the withholding tax during World War II.)

Colorful language has been used successfully by a few specialists, but even the best of them have a tendency to overdo it and end up straining. The very best humor writers usually avoid dependence on verbal acrobatics, and the handful of journalists who have made colorful language their trademark generally are at their best on the occasions when they have something serious to say and use straightforward, simple language. (Humor, of course, is the most difficult form of writing and requires a master's touch. It can be painfully irritating when not done superbly well.)

In business writing, style should never call attention to itself. Words are a means to an end. They should be servants, not masters. Use them functionally to convey your meaning clearly and forcefully and forget about colorful and unusual similes, metaphors, and other types of expressions. Even if you have hit upon what may strike you as a particularly felicitous phrase, regard it with suspicion. Let it stand if it still gives you pleasure at a second or third reading, but be ruthless about deleting it if it does not.

This does not mean that your writing should always be formal. You can be loose, casual, informal—even chatty if this fits the purpose of your communication. But do avoid cuteness, slang, jargon, deliberate regionalisms, and far-out expressions. Usually these are not acceptable even when you put them in quotes.

Quotation Marks

I should have put the expression "in quotes" between quotation marks. "Between quotation marks" is the correct, formal phrase, whereas "in quotes" is a shorthand expression. I didn't do it because I don't like using quotation marks for any expression that is merely colloquial. It may frequently be better not to use such an expression; but when we do, let's own up to it and carry it off without obliquely assuring our readers that we really know better. Frequently quotation marks convey the impression that we are apologizing for a convenient expression that isn't quite "up to snuff"—see what I mean? I shouldn't use "up to snuff" at all, and I wouldn't have used it except to demonstrate the abuse of quotation marks. If you want to use slang and feel you can justify its use, then use it without apology and quotation marks. If you cannot justify its use, then find a different expression. Quotation marks are mainly for quoting someone or something, or for setting something off, not for being arch, diffident, or genteel.

When you introduce a new or unusual expression and intend to use it throughout, you can place it in quotes the first time and drop the marks thereafter. The Government Printing Office Style Guide lists nine instances when quotation marks are used, and nine when they are not. Consult this or any other style guide for the technically correct use of quotation marks.

33 ✍ Elegant Variation

Fowler scorns as "elegant variation" the practice of substituting a new word for one previously used in order to avoid being repetitious. This widespread practice is merely annoying in ordinary writing but can become a serious problem in technical, legal, and other types of writing where precision is of the essence. A writer will use the word "device" two or three times in a row and then get tired of it and call the device a "unit," raising doubt in the reader's mind whether or not the writer is still talking about the same subject. Or a writer will talk about a "derrick" in the first part of a paragraph and switch to "hoist" in the next. Or he'll inject ambiguity by substituting a pronoun to avoid repeating a noun or a name.

The desire to break the monotony of repeating the same word several times is laudable, but it should be suppressed if it results in confusing the reader. Often we simply cannot help repeating the same word. The following examples show how ambiguities can result from elegant variation.

The president of the company told the sales manager that the chairman of the board had been well pleased with *his* report. (*His? Whose?* The sentence should probably read "... had been well pleased with the sales manager's report.")

Adjust the volume using the POWER control. Turn the *knob* slowly clockwise ... (What knob? Why not "Turn the control ..."?)

The law against possession of marijuana provides severe penalties against offenders. It may be unjust; it may be over severe. But it is the law. And a person violating the *statute*. ... (It may sound better, but why switch from law to statute? People may ask themselves if there is a difference between law and statute. And they may wonder if the writer is still talking about the same thing or about another law, called a statute.)

34  Miscellaneous Confusions

Shall/Should/Would

"Shall" is prescriptive, used mainly in a legal context and in specifications. It enjoins compliance. "Should" is weaker, recommending and requesting rather than enjoining action. "Will" indicates future action, agreement, compliance. The three verb forms must not be used interchangeably. Examples:

> Contractor shall furnish bond to ensure timely completion of the job. (Buyer's contract specification.)

> We will furnish completion bond in the amount of $10,000, to be deposited. ... (Contractor's acceptance of specifications.)

> You should request contractor to furnish a completion bond ... (Recommendation by a third party.)

Past/Present/Future

In most expository writing, there is little valid opportunity for using the past tense. Use present tense whenever possible. Future tense is usually unnecessary. Past tense is frequently wrong.

Can/May

"Can" means capability. "May" implies choice.

Effect/Affect

"Effect" used as a noun means "result"; used as a verb, it means "bring about" or "make happen." "Affect" is used as a noun only in psychology. The common use of "affect" as a verb is "to influence, bring about a change." You are usually safe using "effect" as a noun and "affect" as a verb.

That/Which

One of the more annoying habits many writers, including good writers, let themselves slip into is to use "which" in place of "that." This is not just a stylistic nicety; it may affect the meaning of what you are saying. "Which" introduces a commenting clause; "that" a restrictive, defining clause.

These are the arguments *which* we have heard before.

This is wrong. The sentence should read, "These are the arguments that we have heard before," because the clause "we have heard before" defines a characteristic of "arguments."

These arguments, which we have heard before, won't be repeated in this paragraph.

Here this same clause "which we have heard before" is commenting instead of defining. It is correctly introduced by "which" and separated from the rest of the sentence by commas.

The distinction isn't always easy to make, but once you develop sensitivity to it, you'll find it difficult to do it wrong. And you'll find the mistakes jarring in your reading. Remember, "which" is for comment; "that" is for restricting definition. The following examples show right and wrong uses, with the correct use and comments given in parentheses.

The garbage truck which has four wheels and flies does not exist. (The garbage truck *that* has four wheels . . . The clause defines a certain type of truck.)

The word "flies," which can either be a verb form or the plural of the noun "fly," is one of the first examples of *double entendre* children are exposed to. (This is correct. The clause is commenting, not restricting, or defining. The sentence would still make sense if the commenting clause were left out altogether.)

The preposition which ended the last sentence is "to." (The sentence would be meaningless without the defining clause. Should be: The preposition *that ended* . . .)

The preposition, which knew it shouldn't be at the end of the sentence, died of shame. (A borderline case depending on the intended meaning.)

Typing is a skill which (*that*) is useful to everybody. (Typing skill is defined.)

There's no use crying over milk which (*that*) is spilled. (Milk is defined.)

✔Milk, which was spilled here every day for the past ten years, has left an indelible stain on the floor. (The clause between commas is explanatory; that is, the commenting parenthetical clause could be left out without changing the meaning of the sentence.)

This spoon, which has been used to make mud pies, is not to be used as a soup spoon. (Same comment as above.)

✔The spoon which (*that*) you left in the cabinet is the one I used to take my medicine. (Spoon is defined.)

Accidents which (*that*) are caused by carelessness are responsible for the high insurance rates. (Accidents are defined. Not all accidents are responsible for high insurance rates.)

Accidents, which are caused by carelessness, never happen to a careful person. (This means that all accidents are caused by carelessness.)

✔The same alibi which (*that*) I've heard a thousand times . . . ("Alibi" is further defined.)

His alibi, which everybody accepted as credible, was that . . . ("Which" clause is commenting—could be omitted.)

The automobile, which I had rented just for the day, broke down before I got on the freeway. (Same comment as above.)

✔The automobile that I rented from XYZ Company broke down. (Automobile is defined.)

These examples should be enough to illustrate the point. You could improve some of these sentences (the ones marked ✔) by leaving out either pronoun, which has the added advantage of eliminating the need for a decision on "that" or "which," though not on whether or not to enclose the clause in commas. "The spoon you left in the cabinet is the one . . ." clearly calls for no commas, but "Milk, spilled here every day . . ." just as clearly requires the commas. The question of punctuation obeys the same rules as the that/which dilemma: separate by commas commenting clauses; integrate, i.e. leave commas out of, defining clauses.

> Bus drivers who are required to sell tickets and make change are frequently rude.

This sentence tells us something about the strains and stresses of a bus driver's working day. If you separate the defining clause ("who are required to sell tickets and make change") by commas, you make it into a commenting clause and turn the sentence into an insult to all bus drivers. Compare the following statements:

> Small children who get much individual attention are always well behaved.
> Small children, who get much individual attention, are always well behaved.

The first statement may or may not be true, but the second statement is patently untrue. If you are in doubt about whether a clause is commenting or defining, read the sentence aloud and listen to your inflections. Usually this will clarify meaning and punctuation.

Part Three

HOW TOs

35 ✍ Using a Word Processor

You don't have to be an engineer to drive a car, and you don't have to be a programmer to use a word processor. In fact, it's easier to use a word processor than to drive a car, since you don't risk life or limb doing it. Both have to be learned but, starting from scratch, learning to operate a word processor takes a lot less time than learning to drive a car. Other than knowing how to type there are no prerequisites. It helps to have someone nearby who can guide you over the rough spots and initial frustrations, but you can learn on your own, largely by following the step-by-step instructions displayed on the video screen.

The general principles discussed in this chapter will serve as an introduction for people considering getting a word processor but uncertain about what they can do with it, or possibly overawed by anticipated difficulties. Briefly, owning a word processor won't automatically improve your writing, but it helps. Word processing has made it easier for me to write fluently, and I find working on a keyboard less tiring than using a typewriter because it's so simple to make changes and corrections.

For me, having a word processor is the answer to a prayer. I'm a writer who continually changes his mind and makes last-minute changes even in the final copy. The word processor lets me do this without the penalty of destroying or messing up clean copy. Most of my writer friends have by now acquired word processors, and even those who have one at the office have bought one to use at home. The unanimous consensus among all of us is that once you get used to working with a word processor, you never go back to the typewriter.

Advantages

What can a word processor do for you? Although I'm not familair with wordprocessing software other than the one I use, IBM's DisplayWrite 3, I believe all systems of similar size are able to let you:

1. Avoid typing second, third, and nth drafts because the system incorporates all corrections, revisions, deletions, and insertions in your original copy and rearranges pages and paragraphs, leaving no evidence of any editing other than what you did on the "hard" copy. The page produced by the printer is always clean.

2. Forgo proofreading of text that was previously proofed. The machine is incapable of making an error in copying what is displayed on the screen. With text or tables produced on a typewriter, minor changes frequently result in major retyping, all of which then has to be proofed again. The word processor completely eliminates the need for retyping and reproofing.

3. Type without paying attention to the right margin. When you reach the end of the line, the system "wraps around" to the next line automatically.

4. Instruct your system to print your copy with an even right margin (right-justified).

5. Erase by backspacing, by using the delete key, or, for blocks of text, by employing a simple delete procedure.

6. Insert characters, words, sentences, or paragraphs by simply typing them in.

7. Replace data by typing the new data over the old.

8. Save portions of text for reuse at a later time.

9. Produce underlining or bold type semi-automatically.

10. Center titles or captions semi-automatically.

11. Merge two different documents, e.g., to produce multiple individualized letters.

12. Have the system check for spelling and typing mistakes. Words misspelled or not in the dictionary are highlighted.

13. Instruct the system to find, highlight, change, or erase words and phrases scattered throughout the document.

14. Have the system insert running heads or feet, as specified.

15. Instruct the system to insert footnotes at the end of a page.

16. Format and reformat the document until you're satisfied with its appearance on the screen.

17. Make drawings, using the system's graphic capability.

18. Keep your files on disk storage. You give each document a file name by which it is recalled when needed. You can then add to, revise, or otherwise manipulate this document. The system displays all file names on command, so you can always find the file you want. For example, you can have a file for your personal résumé, update it whenever there is a change, and always have it ready for printout at the touch of a button. Correspondence, financial records, different versions of report drafts—all can be kept in storage on disk without risk of loss.

   In addition to the 18 capabilities mentioned above, many others may be available, for instance tabular work and arithmetic operations.

This Is How It Works

Most word processors are "menu-driven," which means that you select the operation you want to perform from various menus that are displayed on the screen. Prompt lines displayed at the bottom of the screen will guide you through the sequence of an operation, and preprogrammed "function" keys generate prompt-line choices and perform certain operations like adjusting ragged lines, presenting you with a "help" menu, displaying a file directory, etc.

Word processors differ in how they get you to the typing area, but once there you can type at will, as freely and as fast as you please, without worrying about making mistakes, overrunning the right margin, returning to the left margin, exceeding page length, or observing any other mechanical constraints imposed by the typewriter.

Whatever you type is "echoed" on the screen where a blinking underscore, called the cursor, tells you where your next keystroke will be placed. The cursor can be moved—by four-directional cursor keys in some systems, by a "mouse" that sits next to the keyboard in others. The cursor is the means for making corrections and manipulating text.

For example, you want to move a paragraph from one page to another. You place the cursor at the beginning of that paragraph and press a function key that is programmed for the command "move." You are then prompted with an on-screen message to "Move cursor to the end of block and enter." You do this and are prompted with another message. "Move where?" After moving the cursor to where you want the block of text inserted, you press the Enter key, whereupon you'll see the paragraph displayed on the screen. The place you moved it from will be automatically filled in by the text that previously followed the moved paragraph. Similarly, if you delete a character, a word, or a sentence, the deleted space is automatically filled in and the lines are rebalanced.

Another example. I have a printer with a continuous paper feed, which doesn't let me use cut paper with my own letterhead. To avoid typing a letterhead each time I start a letter, I typed it once and saved it with a simple command that lets me recall it any time I need it when I start a new letter.

It Takes Patience

The word processor is a powerful tool indeed. It can't do the writing for you, but it can do almost everything else. But do arm yourself with patience, because it takes some time to learn the system and work it with ease. Don't expect to switch from typewriter to word processor without some initial frustration and loss of tempo. Don't switch while you're under pressure. Wait for calmer times to learn to use the system.

I experienced difficulties and frustrations when I first switched from typewriter to word processor. I hit the carriage return key when I shouldn't have and ended up with broken lines that I didn't know how to splice together again. I failed to observe the status line at the top of the screen and replaced characters when I wanted to insert them and vice versa. I made typing errors specifying a file name and became infuriated when the system refused to honor my request. I made lots of mistakes because I was impatient and found it too boring to look at the documentation. None of this was the fault of the system.

After less than a week I settled down and began to use it efficiently. I still hadn't learned all the fine points, but I knew enough to produce clean, error-free, properly formatted copy, and felt free to make changes as extensively and as often as I wanted to. A miracle!

36 ✍ Letters and Memos

Letters are addressed to the outside world; memorandums, or memos for short, are internal communications. What both have in common is that they're communications between human beings, not between organizations. They should always retain the human touch. Business letters and memos need not be dry, impersonal, stiff, or stuffy. Don't hesitate, for example, to use the personal pronouns "I," "we," "you," or to write "we're" for "we are," "can't" for "cannot," "it's" for "it is"; and try to inject a degree of spontaneity into your writing, even at the expense of some rough edges. Warmth, sincerity, and friendliness will, in a pinch, overcome awkward prose.

To insure success in your letters and memos, remember these additional DOs and DON'Ts:

BE DIRECT: Come straight to the point. Say what you have to say in a straightforward way. Although a certain amount of "buffering" may be necessary to avoid the appearance of abruptness, this should not be overdone.

BE PROMPT: A prompt response, even it its wording isn't perfect, is better than one that's late and polished.

BE COMPLETE: Cover all details; answer all questions; ask every question to which you need an answer; date your communication; and cite all required references.

BE BRIEF: Say all that has to be said, but don't try your reader's patience by going on and on. Don't repeat what was said in the communication you answer, don't give information that is not to the point.

Above all, avoid souring relationships:

DON'T ACCUSE, DON'T NEEDLE: Avoid using phrases like

> You are quite wrong in thinking . . .
>
> You misinterpreted . . .
>
> You failed to appreciate . . .
>
> You couldn't help but understand . . .
>
> If, as you say, you actually did . . .
>
> I cannot believe that . . .
>
> You're being unreasonable in . . .

DON'T BE CONDESCENDING: Avoid sounding like a stuffed shirt by writing things like

> We give you permission to use our wording of . . .
>
> Although it appears unlikely to us that our equipment actually failed, a firm of our stature need not quibble over such a small matter . . .
>
> After you've read the literature, you may call me at . . . .
>
> You evidently don't realize that we've been in the data processing business for 15 years . . .
>
> A banking institution of our status doesn't deal with the kind of loans you've applied for . . .

DON'T BE SARCASTIC: They may sound funny to you, but the reader won't be amused by phrases like

> Could page 27 of the contract be missing? It says right there in black and white that . . .
>
> We realize, of course, that long division can present problems, but with hand-held computers readily available, it should be possible . . .
>
> We regret that we're not an eleemosynary institution . . .

DON'T PREACH, DON'T TEACH: Readers don't appreciate being instructed as in

You need to update your inspection procedures . . .

You will not solve the problem of your production bottleneck unless you . . .

This would not happen if you handled your incoming correspondence as we handle ours. What we do is . . .

Let me explain to you how you should do this in the future.

DON'T BRAG: Let facts and figures speak for themselves. Avoid empty boasts like

Our small band of dedicated scientists is capable of . . .

Our team of scientists and engineers is recognized for its unique expertise in . . .

In a huge, multinational corporation like ours, auditing controls are all but foolproof . . .

DON'T BE RUDE: Avoid statements that offend like

The brochure you requested is enclosed. Next time address your request to Stockholders Relations.

Your application for employment has been rejected. Your experience and qualifications are insufficient.

We thought you signed this contract in good faith.

We entered the negotiations assuming you could be trusted.

Failure to avoid any one of these missteps can do you or your company lasting harm. Clarity, precision, and conciseness are all very well, but they won't do you a bit of good if you are accusing, needling, condescending, sarcastic, preachy, teachy, bragging, or rude.

Letters: How to Get Results and Avoid Calamities

Whenever you write a letter, you must have a clear idea of what you want to accomplish by writing it. That's easy if you simply ask for, or furnish, information. But it becomes difficult if you want to soothe upset egos, clear up a misunderstanding, change somebody's mind, or, hardest of all, get action.

Strategies

There are many ways to achieve these ends, many of them better than writing a letter, but a letter is frequently the only means you have and you must make the most of it. In devising your strategy, bear in mind that you will make an impact on the emotional as well as the intellectual level. To reach the intellect, you have to do all the things you do in all other communications: be clear, coherent, concise, and to the point. As we've seen in previous chapters, that's not always easy but it's manageable. Making the desired impact on the emotional level, though, can be difficult.

Be Aware of Your Own Emotions

One difficulty is that you're usually involved emotionally yourself. You may wish to justify an action for which you were criticized, but end up sounding defensive; you intend to clear up a misunderstanding and make it worse by insisting that it really wasn't a misunderstanding and that you were right all along; you try to apologize for something and sound too weak, being more contrite than may be good for you; you may have to tell someone to get off your back and find it difficult to strike the right balance between being firm and being abrupt; you may want to say "thank you" and overdo it; or something more difficult, "no, thank you," without giving offense.

There are no simple prescriptions for handling these situations other than to be aware of the emotional component in your writing and to check your letter carefully to make sure that what you write doesn't do you more harm than good.

One other situation needs special attention. When you're burned up, when you're really angry, that's the time to write a letter. Don't mail it, mind you! But do write it. Get all the poison out of your system. Then throw the letter away. Or at least let it simmer for a few days. Ask yourself, What will I accomplish by sending it? Will it do anything for me other than turn the recipient into a lasting enemy?

Writing an angry, indignant letter may at times be necessary. It may bring results by showing that you've been the victim of injustice. Most people want to think of themselves as fair and just and may do things to preserve that self-image. But letters that get results are seldom written in the heat of anger. We all enjoy writing these letters. But we should never send them without carefully weighing the consequences. Angry words said face-to-face can be taken back a moment later. Hurtful words set down on paper cannot be taken back.

Consider Your Reader's Emotions

Just as your own emotions are involved in writing a letter, your recipient's feelings are equally involved in reading it. Always put yourself mentally in the other person's position. Playwrights call this empathy, the ability to see the world through another person's eyes. Textbooks on business letters usually call it the "you" attitude. It means that instead of being preoccupied with your own problems and concerns, you should bear in mind what impact your problem will have on your reader. My friend Applebaum was pacing the floor one night, unable to go to sleep. "What's the matter?" his wife asks. "Why can't you go to sleep?" "I owe Moriarty $10,000. It's due tomorrow and I haven't got the money." "So call him up and tell him," Mrs. Applebaum says. "What good will that do?" he asks. "Now Moriarty won't sleep. But you will." That's an example of the "you" attitude. Always consider the impact your message is likely to have on its receiver.

Once you adopt this stance, you'll use "you" more often than "I" or "we" without even trying. A letter that addresses itself to my concerns will involve me infinitely more than one mainly concerned with yours. And if it's really your concern alone and not your reader's, a little stroking of your correspondent's ego will rarely do you any harm. In today's mail I found the average load of four solicitations (italics mine):

> It gives me great pleasure to send *you* information about the upcoming Celebrity Series. *You* are invited to join us.... Here is what *you* will enjoy ...

> If *you* saw the Academy Awards, *you* shared our pride as the Wiesenthal Center film won the coveted Oscar....

> One of the added benefits *you* get by having a Texaco Credit Card is an opportunity to shop right from *your* arm chair.... *Your* Texaco Credit Card makes it possible for *you* to enjoy some of the most thrilling merchandise available—all designed to make *your* life easier and more enjoyable.

> What is the most effective step that *you,* as a private citizen, can take to bring about the long-overdue nuclear arms freeze?

Each of these solicitations could be shortened and made less wordy. Simply leave out "you" and "your." But they would be less effective. Let's see:

> Our upcoming Celebrity Series will include ...

> We were proud to win ...

> Armchair shopping for some of the most thrilling merchandise available, designed to make life easier and more enjoyable, is one of the added benefits provided by the Texaco Credit Card.

> What is the most effective way to bring about a nuclear arms freeze?

In writing a report, you would probably choose the shorter version. But in a letter designed to get action, to get your reader to write a check, you have to involve him or her on a personal, emotional level, and you do this as it's done in the first versions. You may not like it. You may grumble each time you receive such a letter. Yet experience has shown that it works.

The Need for Tact

Stroking has to be done well, of course. If it's done clumsily, it can easily backfire. A basic requirement, therefore, for writing a good letter is tact. It's a quality that's almost indefinable. The hoary anecdote about the chief steward on a luxury cruise ship will illustrate it. He called his crew together. on the first morning out and admonished them always to be tactful. "Can anybody tell me what I mean by 'tact'?" he asked. A hand shot up. "Yes, Jackson." "This morning," Jackson explained, " I had a chance to exercise tact. I carried a breakfast tray into one of my staterooms, and there was this young honeymoon couple locked in, ahem, a fond embrace." "And what did you do?" "As I said, I used tact. I put down the tray, said, 'Your breakfast, gentlemen,' and walked out."

Tact, in short, is knowing how to avoid embarrassing people, and how to keep your foot out of your mouth. Jackson didn't have it. Some people never learn it. But the lucky few who are gifted with tact have a chance to go far. Sensitize yourself to the effect your letter will have on the recipient and examine each letter from that point of view. The effort will pay you back many times over.

Tone Is Important

Closely related to tact is tone. Finding the right tone is an important part of letter-writing strategy. Some of the pitfalls in adopting the wrong tone are shown in the introduction of this chapter. Many otherwise competent writers come a cropper by failing to strike the right tone.

Different situations and different people demand differences in tone. Having control over the tone you want to use means knowing when to be sober and terse, as, for example, when writing to the military, or when to be loose, casual, and colloquial, as when writing to someone with whom you are on friendly, easy terms. It means knowing when to be respectful without being obsequious, when to be firm, when warm and friendly, when cool, and even when to be hostile. Most of the time, you'll want to sound warm, friendly, and sincere. If you know how to inject these qualities into your letters, you'll be forgiven most other sins. Conversely, the best ideas expressed in the most lucid prose are apt to be rejected if they've couched in language that is haughty, cold, and arrogant.

Examples

Here are some examples of good and bad letters:

If you'd made it clear what you wanted to know in your first letter, there would have been no need for a second one because I would have given you the correct information in my first reply. If you'll reread your first letter, you'll see that it was very confused. We're not supposed to guess what a customer wants to know. We need precise information. You'll find the answers to your questions in the attached listing.

This is an extremely rude letter that serves no purpose other than to put the customer's nose out of joint. It would be better to write:

We're sorry we caused you delay and inconvenience by misunderstanding your first request for information. I hope that the attached listing will answer all your questions. Please call me, or write, if you need any further information. Again, I'm sorry about the misunderstanding.

This letter avoids the irrelevant argument over who is right and who is wrong, repairing any damage that might have been done by the earlier misunderstanding. Here is another example of defensiveness in justifying a mistake that will compound the damage already done.

You were advised when you placed your order that we had no personnel available to produce a manual for the new machine imported from Italy. You insisted, however, that you couldn't use the machine without an English version of the operations manual. In order to help you out, an outside translator/technical writer was engaged who, unfortunately, was unfamiliar with the technical vocabulary and mistranslated several procedures which, you claim, resulted in a stoppage of the operation of the machine. It is regrettable that this happened, but you will recall that we offered to train one of your people on our premises, an offer which you chose to decline. If you'd been willing to wait a few weeks, we could have had the manual translated by one of our own personnel, but you were in a hurry to put the new machine into operation, which forced us to go to an outside agency. You say we should have checked the work for accuracy, but you just didn't give us enough time. Should a similar situation arise again, we simply shall not allow ourselves to be pressured into promising compliance with requirements that simply cannot be met.

Again, this is a totally counterproductive letter. The tone is cold and argumentative, with the words "you claim" offering a gratuitous insult by questioning the customer's truthfulness. A better way to handle this would be to write something like:

We're sorry you've been held up and inconvenienced by misinformation contained in the operations manual for the Impresa Tre. As you know, this is a brand-new machine we're importing from Italy. The one you have was the first of its kind, shipped to you directly from the docks. We had the operations manual translated in advance and had no way of physically checking its accuracy. The manual is currently being revised and we'll send you a photocopy of the draft as soon as it's ready to go to the printer. We hope this will help.

Again, please accept our apologies for the delay you encountered in putting the machine into full operation.

Another letter that can do only harm instead of good is this one by the translator.

What would you have wanted me to do? Hire an engineer at my own expense? For the money you paid me I couldn't afford to do that. I work with the most up-to-date dictionary, but one also needs technical expertise to arrive at the precise translation. In the absence of your personnel providing this expertise, there was nothing I could do other than what I did do, which was to type on the top of the first page "NOT CHECKED FOR TECHNICAL ACCURACY BY ENGINEERING PERSONNEL."

I would strongly advise you that, next time you need a technical translation, you get an engineer with an Italian background to do the work. His English grammar may not be so good, but he'll be strong on all technical points.

This snide, petulant letter will accomplish nothing but to anger the client. A more tactful and diplomatic response would be something like this:

I understand that you're very dissatisfied with my translation of the operations manual for the Impresa Tre planing tool. I've been told that it's not usable in its present form, being full of inaccuracies that have caused the machine to be misused and become inoperative.

I'm sorry and embarrassed that this has happened but must remind you that I accepted the assignment reluctantly and only with the understanding that an engineer from your firm would be available to advise me, and check on, the technical accuracy of my work. Despite repeated requests on my part over a period of three weeks, no technical liaison was assigned to me and I finally delivered the translation with the caution "NOT CHECKED FOR TECHNICAL ACCURACY BY ENGINEERING PERSON-NEL" typed on top of the front page. I would have made any corrections pointed out to me, but no question was ever raised.

This is a dignified letter that points out an evident injustice done to the writer, and does so without spitefulness.

Here are two examples of letters that achieved the desired results. The first was addressed to the president of the California Public Utilities Commission and resulted in a cancellation of a service charge.

General Telephone has billed me $55 for a service call to take care of a disturbance which, it turned out, was caused by a cordless telephone I own. I don't question that the company is entitled to this charge. I do question the manner in which I was entrapped into making the service request.

I purchased the telephone last February and, at the time, asked the operator if official notification was necessary. I was told that it was not. There had been no publicity about it then and I was totally unaware that 1) the cordless phone could in any way interfere with regular service, and 2) that I would be charged $55 if I requested service and the disturbance was then traced back to the cordless phone.

I understand there are literally millions of instruments now being purchased that were formerly leased. Wouldn't it be a simple matter to enclose a notice with each billing advising customers of their potential liability? Wouldn't it be even simpler to have the operator who answers requests for service tell the customer then and there, on the telephone, that there could be this charge? I might have thought twice about requesting service and might have figured it out on my own that my cordless phone was causing the trouble. And if I had not, and then requested service all the same, I would have no complaint now.

There is something punitive in the way the telephone company is handling this matter. I don't blame them for being angry about the invasion of "foreign" instruments. But fairness demands that there should be a warning about service charges.

The next letter resulted in a partial refund of a bill that had already been paid.

My wife paid your bill in full while I was still at the hospital, and I now find out that my insurance will pay only part of it, whereas it paid the full amount for two subsequent operations I had a month later at the same hospital, both using a different anesthesiologist, Dr. George Kellog. Why should your charge, on a per-minute basis, be higher than his?

Dr. Kellog came to see me and check on my condition before and after each operation. You did not. He managed to drop the tube down my throat with enough skill to spare me serious post-operative discomfort. You did not. In fact, although the one where you attended was the shortest of my three operations, my throat hurt like hell for three days afterwards.

I would appreciate a refund of $75, the difference between what I paid you and what the insurance allowed.

Against expectations, I received a check by return mail. The letter seems to have hit the proper note of indignation.

No valid purpose would be served in giving more examples. With routine correspondence, the message is more important than the medium. With nonroutine letters, the writer must be guided in each case by subject matter and circumstances.

Formats

As for length and format, there are no set rules. If you write a report in the form of a letter, it may easily run to several pages, although common sense dictates that a report that's more than two or three single-spaced pages long should be submitted as a separate document with a brief letter of transmittal. Avoid being wordy, but don't omit saying anything that ought to be said just because you want to get everything on one page.

Formats, too, may vary unless they are dictated by a company style guide. When you write a personal letter, take care to give it a pleasing appearance, leaving plenty of white space and writing paragraphs of manageable, nonintimidating length. Salutations present difficulties when you don't know the name of the person you're writing to, and when you don't know if the person is a he or a she. If the letter is important, try to find out the name (and correct spelling), by telephone if necessary. I go to some lengths to avoid the awkward "Dear Sir or Madam" and have adopted a rule of omitting the salutation altogether when addressing an institution like a utility or an insurance company. This practice, though, has not yet found universal acceptance.

Sign-Off

The sign-off presents no problem, except that modern practice frowns on the participial lead-in clause: "Hoping to . . . ," or "Trusting that . . ." etc. before "Yours," or "Yours truly," or "Sincerely," or "Sincerely yours," or whatever form you fancy. But this is important: If your letter is intended to result in some form of action, as most letters are, don't be content to let the letter simply *imply* such action. *Spell it out.* In your last paragraph, either ask your correspondents to take the desired action, or tell them what you will do yourself to relieve them from any need for action.

Here are some examples:

Since I'm hard to reach during the day, I will call your secretary for an appointment.

P.S. On the reverse side, please jot down the names of some friends who would like to learn about KCET. Then return this letter in the enclosed envelope. You can also use this envelope to send additional contributions.

Enclosed is your order coupon. Simply complete it and return it to us in the postage-free envelope.

You'll find the details of the Center's new program in the enclosed letter. I urge you to read that letter and to respond immediately.

Your subscription expires with the next issue. You can insure uninterrupted service by mailing your check immediately in the enclosed envelope.

Because I'll be away from my desk for the rest of the week, I'll call you next week for an appointment so that we can discuss my proposition in greater detail.

A Plea for Civility

Let me add one more plea. Courtesy, graciousness, civility are as important in letters as they are in personal contact, if only to make the competitive pressures we encounter each day easier to bear. One of the imperatives included in civility is promptness in replying to inquiries. Another blessing of civility is graciousness. When someone has done you a favor, respond by sending a note of appreciation. It will be appreciated.

In conclusion, before sealing and sending an important letter, ask yourself these questions:

1. Have I made my meaning clear beyond doubt?
2. Have I covered all necessary details?
3. Have I answered all questions?
4. *Have I avoided giving offense?*

The Memorandum

The memorandum—memo for short—is far and away the most widely used type of business communication. It differs from the business letter in that it is almost exclusively an internal document, not generally used for communicating with the outside world. Therefore, you can omit the formalities that usually go with a letter and concentrate on the substance of your message alone.

Format

The format of the memo is utterly simple. Most companies have preprinted forms, but if you don't have one handy, you can easily duplicate it on the typewriter. You don't even need the word "Memorandum" that is normally at the top of the form; all you do need are these four lines:

TO: (Name of person addressed)   DATE:

FROM: (The writer)

SUBJECT: (A brief descriptive statement on what the memo is about)

You use no salutation (Dear so-and-so) and no sign-off (Sincerely yours), but simply sign your initials either over your name at the top, or at the bottom of the memo. Also, at the end of the text you indicate to whom you are sending copies, a standard practice because the information in a memo is usually of interest to many people in the organization, not just the one addressed. The people to whom copies are sent are listed in alphabetical order unless there is a distribution list, in which case the applicable list is given, e.g., "Distribution C."

Memos are usually single-spaced and may be as short as a two-line announcement to your staff that you'll be away from your office for a given length of time during which so-and-so is authorized to act on your behalf, or as long as the several hundred pages of the famous memo written by mathematician John von Neumann that set in motion the development of the first digital electronic computer during World War II.

Although there is obviously no such thing as an "average" or "recommended" length for a memo, most memos will not be over one page long. This is so because (1) memos are addressed to people who usually require no lengthy background information; (2) they are intended to provide only information, not opinion, justification, or generalities; and (3) they should be limited to one subject, and one subject only. Which brings us to the importance of the subject line.

Subject Line

By stating the subject of your memo at the top, you commit yourself in advance to what you will, and will not, discuss in the body. This has the virtue of warning you against rambling. In a short memo, like the one announcing your temporary absence from the office, you may well be tempted to add that status reports are due on the day you expect to be back. There's no great harm in that except that it will make the subject line look awkward: "Absence from Office and Status Reports." You could, of course, drop the subject line altogether, which would not be considered a federal offense in this case, but since the subject line is the topic of the paragraph, let's assume that you won't. Therefore you'll write two separate memos, one with the subject line "Absence from Office" and the other, "Status Reports Due."

The word "due" was added to make the line more descriptive of what the memo is intended to accomplish. Like the headline of a newspaper, the subject line must give a capsule description of what's in the body of the memo. It, too, must be concise, but not so concise that it's static and fails to inform. Instead of writing "Customer Complaints," it may be better to say "Improper Handling of Customer Complaints"; instead of "Computer Malfunctions," "Working Time Lost Due to Computer Malfunctions"; instead of "XYZ Corporation," "Troubleshooting Snags at XYZ Corporation." Preferably the subject line should be short, but in many cases you'll have to opt for a longer and more descriptive subject line in order to catch your readers' interest and arouse their concern.

Text

The primary purpose of all memos is to inform. They are directed to busy readers overburdened with reading material and must, therefore, catch their interest quickly, get to the point without delay, and be as brief and unadorned as possible. Deductive structure, stressed throughout this book, is essential in a memo. Don't try to buffer bad news by giving explanations first. Give the heart of the matter first, then explain. And any memo that is longer than two paragraphs should have a summary paragraph introducing the rest. As for choice of words and "communicative attitude," all that has been said before on these topics applies equally to memos.

Although the memo is by its nature an unadorned type of communication, it need not be austere and shouldn't be impersonal. Warmth, directness, and sincerity are as desirable in a memo as they are in a letter. Abruptness and an appearance of being opinionated and inflexible will be as grating in a memo as in personal contact. Above all, be clear. Don't let your quest for conciseness lead you to write prose so dense that it becomes difficult to penetrate. Keep your writing loose and free of jargon, even in an interoffice memorandum intended mainly to inform your colleagues.

The two examples at the end of this chapter are both serviceable memos. Notice the subtle difference in tone between the two. The first, written by a manager to lower-level employees, is firmly directive. Tom Johnson expects his orders to be obeyed. Chairman Mulligan's memo is equally firm in substance, but he doesn't take it for granted that his orders will be followed just because he is the chairman. Although administratively at a higher level than his colleagues, he is in every other respect their peer. They are all professional people—university professors—who can't be simply told to do things in a certain way. They have to be reasoned with and persuaded. In a memo as in a letter, tone has to be controlled.

Illustrations

If tables, diagrams, or graphs must be used to illustrate, explain, support, or simplify the text, they should be treated as they are in a report. That is, bulky documentation should be removed from the text proper and appended. Also, avoid using illustrations that serve only as window dressing.

Examples

TO: Technical Service Personnel   DATE: 9-9-85

FROM: Tom Johnson

SUBJECT: Handling of Customer Complaints

In an effort to be helpful, some service people have been trying to handle customer complaints on their own. DO NOT DO SO. All customer complaints must be referred to the salespeople assigned to those accounts. They alone are in a position to handle complaints. Notify them immediately. Do not try to take care of the matter yourself, no matter how trivial it may appear.

Although all of us are expected to maintain good customer relations, the service representatives will not be able to achieve their productivity goals if they become involved in customer problems. These should be handled by the salespeople, not you technical people. Your time is too valuable to be spent on anything other than servicing equipment.

Under no circumstances should customers be referred to Zone, Major Branch, or Headquarters personnel. To repeat, refer complaints to salespeople, and do so without delay.

TO: English Department Faculty   DATE: 12-16-85

FROM: Graham Mulligan, Chairman

SUBJECT: DUE DATES OF FINAL GRADES

All of us, I'm sure, are concerned about the December 30 deadline by which final grades must be submitted. However, I've talked to the registrar, who says there is no possibility of extending this date. Spring registration is earlier than usual this year and, for students to receive final grades before they register for the spring semester, THE GRADES MUST BE SUBMITTED BY DECEMBER 30. As you know, grades are due within five school days after the final exams, according to university policy. Thus December 30 already allows additional days beyond this five-day limit.

Let me repeat: WE HAVE NO ALTERNATIVE. If necessary, you may have to change your final examination plans in order to complete grading and submit grades by December 30, 4:00 p.m.

Many problems will be created if grades are not submitted by the deadline. If you have any questions, please see me.

Copy: Dean Mitchell.

37 ✍️ Report and Proposal Writing

Reports and proposals are in many ways similar. Both are documents that are written to convince, reports as much as proposals. To achieve this goal, both must be factual and informative in content, sober and unemotional in tone, and devoid of rhetoric in style. Both must be responsive, or at least relevant, to the reader's needs and concerns. Both must hold the reader's interest by being well organized and avoiding turgid, overly technical language. And both must incorporate recommendations leading to specific actions: to award a contract to the proposer or, in the case of the report, to adopt the recommended policy or course of action.

In sum, the difference between a proposal and report is in the results they aim for: A successful proposal will result in a contractual relationship that is of direct, material benefit to the proposer, whereas a successful report will result in actions and decisions that are of no direct, material benefit to the writer but reflect his or her findings, convictions, beliefs, or point of view.

Proposal Writing

A proposal is an offer to perform services. It may be nothing more elaborate than a letter proposal, reflecting little special effort, or it may be the end product of thousands of man-hours, consisting of dozens of volumes and running into millions of words. But regardless of size, form, or effort, all proposals are directed toward one goal: to persuade someone to let you, the offeror, perform some specified services on a contractual basis. Regardless of size and form, all proposals basically contain the same functional parts: (1) an introduction and summary of conclusions; (2) a statement of the problem you propose to solve; (3) a statement of the work you will perform to solve the problem; (4) your management approach and performance schedule; and (5) a statement of your capabilities and qualifications for the job. Cost is usually kept separate from the main body of the proposal on the theory that the major variable to be evaluated is the quality of the work, and that cost should not directly influence this evaluation.

Introduction and Summary of Conclusions

This is always the most difficult part to write and frequently the most important because it is the only part that will be read by all of the people who will make the ultimate decision on who gets the contract. Whereas the body of the proposal is usually directed to technical specialists, the introduction is addressed to generalists who want to get the broad picture quickly and painlessly. Therefore, you must (1) articulate the approach you are taking—what might be called the theme of your proposal; (2) present your reasoning, stripped—as far as possible—of technical detail; (3) state your understanding of the problem; (4) summarize how you propose to solve the problem; and (5) summarize the reasons why you, and not one of your competitors, should be given the contract. In other words, the introductory part should summarize the contents of the proposal and give readers a frame of reference by which they can orient themselves. It should tell them what they can expect to find in detail in the body of the proposal. It should *not*, however, be simply a summary of the table of contents.

Summarizing the table of contents is the easy way out of a difficult job. It must be avoided. The introduction must be interpretive. It must explain why one aspect is treated in detail and another is not, why one approach was selected and another dropped. It must reflect every aspect of the proposal, but reflect it in summary form. With a well-written proposal, it should only be necessary to lift the introductory paragraphs of each section and assemble them in the introduction; in practice, things rarely work out that easily. A great deal of labor in digesting and summarizing is hardly ever avoidable.

Although the introduction should be the last part of the proposal to be written in final form, it should be the first to be written in draft form so that it can give focus and direction to the writing effort. You can do this by discussing the problem, sketching approaches on how to solve it, debating alternatives, and anticipating conclusions. It doesn't matter that both the problem statement and the conclusions will probably be revised and reworked several times during the course of the proposal effort. What does matter is that both goal and obstacles be clearly articulated, and that there be an objective toward which individual efforts can be directed.

Statement of the Problem

A detailed statement of the problem should always be the starting point of your proposal. Every proposal is directed toward the solution of a problem, and understanding the problem is a requirement for solving it.

Most proposals are written in response to a request for proposal (RFP), which usually states the problem for which the requestor seeks a solution. In responding, there is always a strong temptation simply to parrot the problem statement as it is worded in the RFP. This temptation must be resisted. Remember that a proposal is an offer to perform services. You are not just giving a quote on an item of merchandise that you can take off your warehouse shelves and ship without delay. Some research, engineering, or manufacturing effort will have to be made before the contract can be fulfilled, or there would be no need for a proposal. You must define the problem from the point of view of the problem solver, then, not just from that of the problem poser, the requestor. Once you view the problem in the proper perspective, you'll find that the two sets of problems are not necessarily identical.

For example, the Air Force may require a lightweight inertial navigation system of extremely small dimensions and high accuracy. It will be helpful, of course, if you can assure them in your first paragraph that you understand the nature of their requirement—i.e., their problem—and are able to satisfy it. But you will give them confidence that you can really solve their problem only if you also show an understanding of your own problem—the difficult engineering involved in fulfilling the specified requirements.

Similarly, a city planning commission may request proposals for the development of a rapid transit system. In your response you may wish to show your understanding of the mounting problems of interurban transportation—congestion, smog, eroding tax bases, downtown parking, etc. This understanding is laudable but beside the point. The planning commission is well aware of these problems. The problem you, as the respondent, are expected to understand and solve is that of designing the best possible transportation system. The two problems are interrelated, of course, but not identical. To be responsive you must concentrate on the total problem from your point of view, not that of the commission.

The two examples show that the two sets of problems are not usually and not necessarily alike. The requestor's problem is something for which he needs and possibly envisages a solution; the offeror's problem consists of the obstacles lying in the path of a solution.

Your statement of the problem, your understanding of the problem, will be an indication of your responsiveness. If you propose an ocean liner to do the job of a tugboat, then you evidently haven't understood the problem and are unresponsive. If you propose a Cadillac for a job calling for a four-wheel-drive Jeep, then again you don't understand the problem. This may seem obvious, but it isn't. Companies that have made analyses of why their losing proposals lost have invariably found that lack of responsiveness was the overwhelming reason. They had proposed an overengineered—and hence too costly—solution for a relatively simple problem. In some cases they had failed to understand the problem altogether, offering oranges where apples were called for.

In proposal evaluations responsiveness is always the primary consideration. The services offered must be within specified requirements. Paradoxically, this is as important in unsolicited proposals as it is in solicited ones. An unsolicited proposal is one in which you anticipate someone's need for your services. The people you direct it to are presumably unaware that the need exists, or they would have taken the initiative and requested proposals. What you must do, therefore, is to make them aware that they have a problem for which you have a solution. In this case, the problem you state will be theirs rather than yours. You yourself must raise the question to which you are responding. You must state the problem before you can hope to get a hearing for your proposed solution.

The situation is similar for scientists looking for research funds. The unsolved problem is, after all, the prime reason for all scientific research. To obtain a grant you must state the problem you propose to solve; a desire simply to collect data isn't enough. Unless you can correlate collecting data and solving a problem, you won't have ammunition to outgun the competition for the funds you're seeking.

An intelligent statement of the problem is one of the most important parts of your presentation. It is the "why" of your proposal—why you are writing it, why you are concerned, why someone should read it.

Work Statement

Next in order of presentation must be *what* you are going to do for your client. In some proposals this is called the work statement, but any other name describing the end product of your efforts will fill the bill. Here you must convince your client that you have investigated every possible avenue of approach and are confident that the approach you've selected is indeed the best. Don't hesitate to marshal all of the facts that either support your case or invalidate an alternative approach. Cite statistics, reports, mathematical proofs, results of computer analyses—anything that has convinced you of the soundness of your own approach. And don't just stop at citing results—prove them. A package of mathematical equations is more convincing than reams of prose assurances. Computer printouts tend to be bulky, but they show that you've done your homework. Of course, you should always place such supporting documentation where it will not directly interfere with the reading process, that is, in appendices or separate sections. In the text itself there should be only results and conclusions, with references to where the proof can be found.

One thing easily lost sight of in technical descriptions is that you are an advocate presenting an argument, the result of hard work and hard thought. You know that it's the best anybody can come up with. Let your conceit show a little. Let it show by giving the reasons why the design approach you have selected is the only one that is fully effective. In other words, make your description functional.

For example, your company may have designed the fuselage of a cargo plane in a certain way to accommodate a specific type of cargo. Don't be satisfied to cite the dimensions of the fuselage but give the reasons why these, and only these, dimensions were chosen. Don't say, "The aisle is six feet wide and ten feet high." Do say, "To provide adequate passage alongside Jeeps stacked one on top of another, minimum aisle space of . . ." Bear in mind the goal of your design and then let every detail support that goal.

Whether the "what" of your proposal is a fund-raising campaign, the development of a complex inertial instrument, or a research project, describing it in terms of what it will accomplish will rescue this part of your proposal from dull passivity. Remember that your proposal is a response to a call for help. What you propose is a solution to a problem. Your readers will repay you by their interest for the trouble you take in pointing your description toward the solution of their problem.

Management

The next point of concern to your client is *how* you're going to manage the contract or grant after you get it. You may feel that this is none of his business, since you are proposing results rather than performance, but the client has legitimate reasons for wanting to know something about your management approach and record. First of all, he wants to have a problem solved, and if you perform badly or late, then even withholding payment won't be much consolation to him, since he's still stuck with the problem. Moreover, most research or development projects are not susceptible to precise, quantitative measurements. Therefore, knowing that your management philosophy is sound can be a major factor in his giving you the nod over your competitor. In some cases management competence can be the decisive factor, outweighing even technical excellence. This will usually be the case with projects running over long periods and requiring the coordination of many people. But even on a research project involving a mere handful of scientists, the contracting agency will want to know how the money is going to be spent and accounted for.

Project management encompasses many questions. First, what sort of organization is going to handle the project? In other words, what is your organization chart? What are the lines of command and authority? Who reports to whom? What power does the organization have in allocating available resources, in terms of facilities, manpower, and funds? If you get the contract, are you going to be shunted over to a corner of the laboratory or factory? Will you have to fight battles for every pencil you want to draw from supplies? This question of organization within an organization is important and needs careful explaining. It can indicate to your client that the project is of great importance to your overall organization and that top management will have a strong interest in seeing it succeed. You must not let your client get the impression that the project is of peripheral interest to your company and that you are bidding on it only from force of habit or on a whim—something not entirely unusual in industry.

All clients are interested in schedules. How long is this job going to take? What are the major milestones? How do you intend to monitor schedules to insure compliance? The assurance of timely performance will weigh heavily in your favor in most projects.

Accounting practices are a point of concern. Frequently proposals are for projects where you spend the client's, not your own, money. The client will be vitally concerned over how you spend it and what controls you intend to use to see that it won't be wasted. This is important even when you spend your own money because a responsible client will not want to see you spend yourself into a hole from which he'll eventually have to help you extricate yourself. A good accounting plan is highly important.

Reporting—both internal and external—is a legitimate concern of your prospective client. What are your plans for keeping him informed of progress—and trouble? Equally important, especially on a large project, are your own internal reporting procedures. Just how do you plan to disseminate information, both from the top down and from the bottom up? Either path can be a major problem in managing a large project, capable of resulting in cost overruns, schedule delays, and similar surprises.

What are your plans for quality assurance? Do you subordinate it to engineering or manufacturing? Or do you regard it as an independent management function under the direct supervision of the project leader? It is something your client will want to know about because your attitude toward this function will reflect on the end product. In a bid for a manufacturing contract, your "reliability plan," including your reliabilty organization, will also be of major importance in an evaluation of your management approach.

Organization, scheduling, cost accounting, reporting and documentation procedures, and quality assurance—these are the major heads under which you must convince your client that you have the requisite management know-how. On a proposal for a modest grant, each of these heads can probably be treated in a sentence or a paragraph. On a bid for a large contract, this section on management can easily run into hundreds of pages, with specialists in each field supplying detailed inputs on work breakdown structures, PERT charts, computerized reports, testing and checking techniques, etc. The section should be an honest reflection of your management philosophy. It usually doesn't pay to give lip service to management fads and sacred cows if you don't believe in them and don't intend to carry them out. Explain how you intend to run the project and why you believe your way is the best way to run it. You may believe either in tight control or in giving associates and subordinates extensive leeway for using initiative. You can argue your case either way. You may believe in managing and keeping informed by telephone or personal contact, or you may prefer detailed documentation and frequent written reports. You can make a case one way or the other.

Let me inject a note of caution before my enthusiasm for honesty gets the best of me. To get the contract you'll want to be responsive to the client's wishes. If he wants tight controls, don't argue in favor of loose procedures. If he wants critical path scheduling, give him his critical path networks. He'll probably spell it out in his RFP; if he doesn't, marketing intelligence can gather this information, or previous contact and experience will tell you what he wants. Whichever way you approach it, be sure to inform your prospective customer just how you intend to manage the job.

Capabilities

The final point that must be covered by your proposal is the question of identity. In many cases you take it for granted that your client knows who you are and is aware of your qualifications for the job. Even so he'll need some documentation, if only to justify his confidence in you to his own superiors. Organizations with established proposal techniques usually have "boilerplate" material, that is, material that can be used again and again with only slight modifications. Some organizations use company brochures to tell their story, although this is not done often because brochures usually lack the tight focus necessary for proposals. A characteristic of boilerplate is that it is flexible and lends itself to selective assembling.

Personnel

The most important asset among your capabilities is, without question, the caliber of people who are going to work on the project. This last qualification is important. The president of your company may be remote to the point of insignificance. Therefore, the inclusion of his or her résumé in your proposal may add little. Similarly, an outstanding scientist on your staff may not be available to your project if his or her time is already spread over three other projects. You may at times be able to get away with using the scientist's name, but you'll have to be careful to maintain credibility. Evaluators will ask themselves, "What is this person doing *now?*" And you'll have to be prepared to give a plausible answer. You may, of course, have indicated in the management section that certain named people will be available to the project on a part-time basis, indicating the percentage of their time they will contribute; but supplying résumés promiscuously without honest intent or expectation of having these people on the project is bad practice and apt to backfire. However, those professional and management people who will work on the project should be named, and named first among your capabilities.

The standard format for listing personnel is to submit their résumés. You need no more than the briefest introduction, stating in one or two sentences the scope, intent, and content of the subsection to follow.

5.1 *Project Personnel*

This section presents résumés in alphabetical order of professional and management personnel who will be assigned to this project or be available to it on a consulting basis. Please refer to Section 4.2, Project Organization, for specific project assignments.

Related Experience

Of almost equal importance in proving your qualifications is your organization's related experience, a standard phrase meaning experience that is directly applicable to the proposed project. Normally this presents no difficulty, since most proposals are generated within reasonably narrow limits of an organization's specialization, but showing related experience may not be so easy when you are trying to move into new or adjacent fields. In this case you'll have to slant and weigh experience to show relatedness.

In describing related experience you should always be specific about the project, the product, the problems encountered and solved, and functions performed. Each important facet of experience should be treated in summary form, and the style should be concise and to the point. Rambling generalities usually betray insecurity and lack of substance.

To inform the requestor of the scope of your related experience, it may be helpful to supply a table summarizing the projects or products cited. For some proposals it may be advisable to develop a matrix of related experience, listing the projects on one axis and project functions on the other and putting Xs in the resulting boxes as applicable.

	System Analysis	Project Management	Protype Development	Production
Project X	X	X	X	
Project Y	X		X	
Project Z		X		X

Proper use of graphics can dress up this section and break up some of the monotony. Airbrush renderings, photographs, charts, and graphs are part of the boilerplate experienced proposal groups use to give their proposals a professional appearance.

Facilities

Part of your capabilities may be represented by your facilities—plant, laboratories, special equipment. You want to assure your client that you are well equipped to handle the job. The narrative description here should be quite brief, with the bulk of information supplied in tabular or graphic form. Again, much of this material can be boilerplate; and what you include, and whether or not you include it at all, will depend on the size and nature of your proposal and, of course, on the relevance of the information supplied. You may want to include items such as

- Assigned space—usually given in square feet, supplemented by a floor plan showing assigned area cross-hatched.
- Computer facilities
- Special equipment—standard manufacturing and laboratory equipment is usually not detailed, but special equipment helpful or essential for doing the job should be listed.
- Other features—air conditioning, climate, proximity to universities, accessibility, etc.

Finally, under capabilities, you may want to cite the availability of a pool of skilled manpower and give an indication of your financial position unless you're at the point of going bankrupt.

Except for appendices, your proposal will normally end with "capabilities." In very short, letter-type proposals, you may end with a brief conclusion and a call for action, but in most proposals this is omitted.

Front Matter

Front matter consists of cover, title sheet, table of contents, preface, and frontispiece. A copy of the letter of transmittal is at times included. It should be factual, giving only pertinent and necessary information.

Cover

The choice of cover is a merchandising decision. Most active proposal groups use very simple covers, some with die-cut windows for the title, others with a reprint of the title page. But the same groups will at times use fancier covers when this seems to be indicated and a good thematic approach is available. The only requirement for a cover is that it be neat and provide identification—title and name of offeror.

Title Sheet

The title sheet is the proposal's formal introduction. It must contain the full name of the proposal, the name of the party to whom the proposal is addressed, proposal date, and the name of the offeror. In addition, the title sheet frequently carries a statement to the effect that the material contained in the proposal is proprietary to the offeror and must not be disclosed in whole or in part without his express consent. The exact wording of the statement will vary from company to company and sometimes from proposal to proposal, but the purpose is always to protect the offeror's proprietary information to the fullest possible extent.

Table of Contents

The table of contents should be arranged for maximum legibility, making it easy for readers to find what they are looking for. In a sectionalized proposal it is usually not necessary to go beyond third subheads, though this may not be enough in very large proposals. A list of illustrations and a list of tables may be added if there is enough time, but these are not of the essence.

Preface

A preface is used to give information for which there is no convenient place elsewhere, like formal administrative information about the proposal, acknowledgments, and restrictive qualifications. Skip it if all you can do is echo the introduction.

Frontispiece

A frontispiece can dress up a proposal. If you have a good photograph or airbrush rendering of something closely related to the subject of the proposal, it will look nice on the page facing the introduction, but it isn't important enough to warrant a lot of trouble or expense.

Back Matter

Back matter includes all appendices and possibly an index. Appendices should contain supporting documentation and other material of possible interest to the proposal evaluator. Common sense usually limits the number of appendices. On a large proposal an index can be extremely helpful in orienting the reader and serving as the necessary cross-reference between related sections. Even if the index contains no more than the information in the table of contents, the fact that the index has it in alphabetized and permuted form will be of great help.

Keep in mind that the proposal is a relatively minor part of the total effort devoted to getting contracts or grants from a customer or client. Successful proposals are usually preceded by other contacts and frequently represent merely the dot on the "i." But proposal writing is an important and costly effort. If you do write a proposal, do it right—a sloppy proposal can do more harm than good.

Report Writing

Like proposals, reports can be long or short, formal or informal; but unlike proposals, reports have no clearly defined parts. The organization of each report is dictated by the material itself, not by formal requirements.

The only structural similarity among different types of reports is that all have a summary of findings/conclusions and recommendations at the head of the body of the report. This is the single organizational must for this kind of report, not a formal requirement but one imposed by the reasons why reports are written and read.

Let's be clear about the type of report we're dealing with. The majority of all reports are financial, administrative, status, and progress reports, submitted for the most part on a scheduled basis and frequently computer-generated. These are not the types of reports we're concerned with here. They are important as vehicles for data and information, but they don't usually convey explicit recommendations. The reports we are concerned with are frequently solicited and always submitted for a special purpose— to take a certain action, adopt a new policy, make changes, or keep things on an even keel. They include feasibility reports, facility reports, research reports, inspection reports, and others, all having the common denominator of evaluating data, reaching conclusions, and recommending action. They may range from the report on the performance record of a vendor to one on your company's communications network, or on the acquisition of a new facility.

Reports are among the most important inputs to the decision-making process; but reports that are poorly written will fail to make the desired impact: they'll be left unread, or be half-read and misunderstood, or be annoying to the point where they'll prejudice the reader against the writer's conclusions, or—the most common fate—be simply put aside and ignored. To avoid any of these possibilities for your reports, follow these recommendations:

1. Know what you want to accomplish by writing the report. This is not as obvious a truth as it may appear to be. In the light of history we may assume that the Warren Report was written to lay to rest public fears of a conspiracy rather than to assert with finality what happened

in Dallas in November 1963. Similarly, if your principal asks you to write a report on what effects certain mandated budget cuts had on the operation of your department, you should be clear on whether he wants to defend the cuts or show how badly they crippled the department.

2. Consider your strategy. As a young man, the late Robert Moses wrote a brilliant and much-acclaimed report on civil service reform in New York City. Despite its brilliance, though, the report almost aborted Moses's career because it stirred up a hornet's nest of opposition. Later Moses became a master of political strategy whose reports accomplished what he wanted them to accomplish. You, too, may at times have to choose between long-range results and a brief moment of glory. For example, if your aim is efficiency and you recommend abolishing jobs, you have to be aware of the concerted opposition you arouse among those who stand in danger of losing their jobs. Good report writers know how to manipulate their material to serve their ends. This isn't dishonest; just good sense.

3. Have a clear conception of who will read your report. If you discover a flaw in something you or your group have developed, it may be important that you report this to your principal with copies to your colleagues. It may not be wise to disseminate the report to others outside your group. On the other hand, in the report on the budget cuts you'd want to keep in mind that it is probably intended to be read by higher levels of management.

4. Give a summary of your conclusions and recommendations early in the report. Don't make your readers wait to the end, or make it necessary for them to turn to the end without reading the body of the report. By summarizing conclusions and recommendations early, you retain a measure of control over your readers.

5. Adopt a tone that is restrained, dignified, and nonsensational. If you want your point of view to prevail, any show of passionate, one-sided partisanship will defeat this purpose. A thoughtful, balanced report reflecting a judicious, impartial attitude will be most effective. Avoid unsubstantiated guesses, unwarranted conclusions, and glossed-over facts and figures. This does not mean that you should qualify every statement or that you should never show enthusiasm and warmth.

6. In a long report, provide an Executive Summary directed to high-level decision makers who do not have the time, the patience, or frequently the technical expertise to wade through the details of the report.

7. Strengthen the "visibility" of the report through good page design and clear organizational breakdown. Provide a table of contents for reports with more than 15 pages, an index for those with more than 50 pages. Detailed documentation should go into one or more appendices where they won't overwhelm readers and break reading stride.

8. Since reports always have relevance to an existing problem or

situation, you'll usually have to sketch in the background before you summarize conclusions and recommendations. Avoid making the background description overlong, though. You're apt to sound defensive about your conclusions if you devote a disproportionate amount of space to matters that don't constitute new information. Background information also interferes with deductive structure.

9.   As in the proposal, always give an introduction that summarizes the entire report.

Besides the body of the report, title and contents pages, an index, and the appendices, you may need an abstract, a preface, and a letter of transmittal. An abstract is mainly for the guidance of potential readers not directly addressed by the report. It is used as an entry in a data bank, allowing readers to scan a large amount of material quickly before deciding what to read in detail. An abstract, therefore, must be extremely concise, usually not more than 100 words. It is always written in the present tense, without embellishments or value statements (i.e., *not* "This is a really good report . . ."). Briefly, the abstract should give (1) purpose and scope of work done, (2) method used, and (3) results, recommendations, and conclusions. No information or conclusion should ever be given in the abstract that is not contained in the report itself.

A preface is used for items such as:

Acknowledgments

Purpose of work on which the report is based

Project authorization

Scope of the report, including limitations due to legal, financial, or time constraints

Identification of team members and collaborators, if any.

("Preface" and "foreword" are almost interchangeable terms, but "foreword" is customarily used for the lengthy introduction of a work by a person other than the author.)

A letter of transmittal is just that: a brief note indicating what report is being sent, why it is being sent to the person addressed, and what it is intended to accomplish. The letter should not be used for salesmanship unless this is done with a great deal of finesse.

Other front and backmatter requirements are similar to those in a proposal.

38 ✍ Editing

At one point or another, many writers find themselves performing editing functions. Editing requires considerable skill: you must know how to write, be well organized, be conscious of details, be able to understand any number of subjects, and be tactful enough to handle touchy authors with care. You may be an otherwise superb editor, but without tact you won't be effective. Your authors will become either intimidated or rebellious, will either dry up or cut your throat. No author worthy of the title is ever indifferent to what an editor does to his work.

The mechanics of editing are straightforward. Appendix A presents a list of standard proofreading symbols used for communicating with the typist or typesetter. The conventions are slightly more rigid for proofing typeset galleys than for typed or handwritten copy because of the physical distance between typsetter and editor. With typed copy, the typist is usually in a position to walk over to the editor's desk to ask for clarification. But proofreading is only one part of the editing function. One of the most important editing functions—working with the manuscript—can be performed independently of any knowledge of mechanics. It requires good sense and orderly habits and, not the least, some feeling for the English language.

The most basic editing function is formatting. The editor decides on or agrees to a proposed format and then is responsible for policing and enforcing it. Format includes structure (division into chapter, sections, subsections); heading subordination; page layout; eliminating repetitive material; treatment of footnotes and cross-references; consideration for stylistic preferences and idiosyncrasies; and standardization of non-text material. Format means, "This is the way we do it here at XYZ Inc."

Arguments over the relative merits and demerits of one format over another are generally futile. It doesn't matter whether you use open punctuation or closed punctuation, periods or right parentheses after enumerators, or whether you call appendices appendixes. What does matter is that whatever you do, you always do it the same way, at least in the same document.

The best way to establish "the way we do it here" is to have a style guide. It should be brief and reserved mainly for exceptions, differences, and special preferences, all with respect to some norm such as the standard style guides (i.e., those published by the University of Chicago Press, the

U.S. Government Printing Office, and the *New York Times*). These standard reference works treat all general questions of style. Topics discussed in individual style manuals may include the following:

1. Rules on abbreviations reflecting editor's stylistic preferences.
2. Special abbreviations not to be found in reference works.
3. Use of acronyms.
4. Rules on capitalization (a constant source of confusion unless ruled on).
5. Captions—where to place them.
6. Special compound words not in standard reference works.
7. Rules for continuing figures and tables to next page.
8. Copyright notification.
9. Cross-references—when, where, how.
10. Special graphics.
11. Special nomenclature.
12. Disclaimer notices.
13. Distribution lists.
14. Editing symbols.
15. Rules on enumeration and subordination.
16. Footnotes—philosophy and mechanics.
17. Figure references—where? how? always?
18. Headings—subordination, type faces, placement.
19. Indentations and margins.
20. Indexing rules.
21. Handling of lists (enumeration, capitalization, punctuation).
22. NOTE, CAUTION, and WARNING—how, when, and where to place the notice.
23. Treatment of numbers (if other than in standard guides).
24. Identification of organizational subdivisions (e.g., chapter, section, subsection, paragraph).
25. Preferences in punctuation.
26. Pluralization.
27. Special procedures.
28. Proofreading procedures.
29. Use of quotation marks.
30. Word usage conventions.
31. Use of symbols—when, where, what.
32. Trademark conventions.
33. Proprietary statement.
34. Anything else you can think of that I haven't mentioned.

Having a style guide will help you to be consistent even if you are the sole editor and the originator of your own rules. But with a multitude of editors and authors all working together, a style guide becomes a necessity. It will also help your authors make life easier for you, and it can save your typing pool a lot of questions. But make it short and easy to use. A style guide that isn't used is not much better than no style guide at all.

Perhaps your most important editing function is your query to the author. In a highly technical context, you may not always be able to understand every detail, and you will be willing to accept the author's premises, derivations, and conclusions on faith; but this does not mean that the logical flow should be beyond your comprehension. Authors can be incoherent, disconnected, and incomplete. As a careful editor you will be able to detect these shortcomings even in technical material you don't fully understand, and you should request clarification. Always go on the assumption that if you don't understand something, another reader may not necessarily understand it either. Time and again you'll find that the question you have been hesitant to ask because it seemed stupid wasn't stupid at all, but was highly justified. This kind of editing cuts to the core of a piece of writing and frequently results in radical revisions. You won't set speed records editing this way, but you will achieve a much improved document.

The more common editorial function is the purely cosmetic one of making the writing and the style more pleasing. This function is important, too, and is usually the one most readily appreciated by authors.

Your most difficult and dangerous function as an editor is rewriting. To do this well, you must be fast, must write well, and must understand thoroughly what you are rewriting. Above all, you must know when *not to rewrite.*

Since most people write badly, some rewriting is usually unavoidable. The danger for the editor to avoid at all costs is to change the author's intended meaning. This defeats the purpose of editing and makes the author very unhappy. There is also the question of hurt pride. No author likes to see his prose cut to shreds and changed beyond recognition. You must ask yourself carefully in each case whether the hurt feelings are worth the improvement, and act accordingly. No material should ever be rewritten or changed for the sake of mere stylistic preference. My own rule as an editor is to let anything pass that is at least adequate. Unfortunately, it is easier to state the rule than to follow it.

Some text has a way of coming apart as a result of even minor changes It's like pulling a loose thread and having the whole fabric start to unravel. I myself haven't always had the wisdom to foresee such calamitous results, spending more time than I should have on relatively minor improvements.

But these are the hazards of editing. To be a good editor takes a talent quite apart from writing talent, and not every writer has the patience, tact, and good judgment to be a good editor. On the other hand, many editors don't have the motivation or special knowledge to be a writer. To work together efficiently, writer and editor must respect each other. And each must be tolerant of the other's shortcomings. It isn't always an easy relationship, but it can be a very rewarding one.

39 ✍ *How to Persuade*

Many scientific and pseudo-scientific studies have been made on the art of persuading people to change their point of view or opinion. The conclusions appear, for the most part, to be intuitively obvious, following a pattern you would expect from a commonsense approach.

Both Sides of Argument?

The first question is whether you present both sides of an argument or only the side you advocate. Basically the answer depends on your integrity, but inasmuch as the entire subject of persuasion is Machiavellian in nature, the aspect of personal integrity should perhaps be left out. In a debate where you can trust the other side to make its own points, you can safely— and without loss of integrity—neglect the opposing arguments and concentrate on your own. But in presenting a written argument you have to take other considerations into account: Who are your readers? How much do they know about the subject? How radical a change do you want to bring about? If your aim is simply to reinforce prevailing opinion, your approach will be different from what it would be if you wanted to defend it against attack, or attack it yourself.

Which Side First?

In attacking a strongly held opinion, you had better bring up the favorable arguments first, to show that you are aware of them, before you start shooting them down. In reinforcing an opinion, you may need only the pros of the argument. In defending an opinion against attack, you will probably use your arguments "for" to defeat the arguments "against."

Still another consideration is the kind of change you wish to accomplish. For a lasting and thorough change of opinion, you'd be well advised to present both sides of the question. For a quick, superficial, emotional change, your argument should also be quick, superficial, and emotional, neglecting all but the most obvious counterarguments.

Admits Bias?

Should you try to hide your own bias in presenting both sides of an argument? To be effective you should appear to be as objective as possible, but not at the cost of seeming hypocritical. If your readers don't believe you, if you appear to lack sincerity, then you've lost the battle before you've started to fight. Readers expect, accept, and excuse advocacy; they will not forgive you for insincerity. You can be a perfect fool and be respected as long as you give the impression of sincerity; you can be brilliant and be despised and discredited if your readers get the impression that you are trying to pull the wool over their eyes.

When you do present both sides of an argument, you should generally present the opposing arguments first and your own last. You gain the advantage of having the last word and leaving the final impression. And it is easier to maintain the dialectical tension by pushing up against an argument than by stating your own and having the counterargument—weaker by definition—push up against it. For the same reason, you should make your most important points first rather than save them for the end. You may reverse this order if you can take lively reader interest for granted, in which case the last point made will carry the heaviest weight. But if you have to arouse interest, then you must hit readers with your most important, your most interesting, points first.

Stress Conclusions?

A standard recommendation for persuasive writing is to "Tell them what you're going to tell them, tell them, tell them what you told them." Despite its hackneyed appearance, this is good advice. Don't take a chance on merely presenting the facts and letting your readers draw their own conclusions. At times these will be so obvious that you can afford to be subtle, and you'll gain by not rubbing your readers' noses in conclusions they can draw for themselves. But most of the time you will be more persuasive if you do your own summarizing and concluding. Similarly, a certain amount of repetition can be a good thing to drive your point home. Most readers are imperfect creatures whose minds skip and wander and miss points they shouldn't miss. Your attentive readers might resent repetition, but they won't forget the source of their irritation. You can be reasonably subtle about repeating a point by varying the way in which you present it—using different illustrations, rephrasing it, or reintroducing it with a deprecatory phrase like "to repeat." But if the point is worth making, it's worth repeating.

Appeal to Authority?

As a final question, you may ask what weight, if any, the appeal to authority has in persuading others. If you can cite someone on your side of the argument who is generally respected and believed, you will obviously predispose your reader in favor of your argument. This will be true even if the person you cite (a movie star or sports hero, for instance) has no specific qualifications for his opinion. Similarly, the consensus of your peers will have a powerful influence, persuading most readers to accept rather than reject. But bear in mind that the appeal to authority is purely a stratagem, a tactic; it is not an argument in itself and cannot and should not take the place of reason and evidence. It may work; it generally will work; but it really ought not to work.

Strategy aside, bear in mind that nothing persuades as forcefully as warmth, sincerity, and enthusiasm. If you can inject these qualities into your writing, you'll need little else to be effective.

40 ✍ *Why and How to Punctuate*

As an experiment, take any randomly selected paragraph and copy it, making no changes other than removing all punctuation marks. You probably will find it confusing, with sentences and thoughts running together without any indication of where to stop and pause. You may have seen this example:

That that is is that that is not is not is that it it is

Even if you've been exposed to it before, you may have trouble figuring out its meaning:

That that is, is; that that is not, is not. Is that it? It is.

The absence of punctuation marks left you with no clue for your inflections, and without inflections the string of words is meaningless. You must separate the words, group them, before they make sense. To bring order out of chaos is to separate. Separating, grouping, is our first step toward understanding; and the first function of punctuation marks is to serve as separators.

Period

The period is the major terminal separator. It terminates a declarative sentence. You use a period to tell your reader that you've come to the end of your statement and that the next word·will start a new one. You don't need a period after a heading because the heading is set off from the paragraph that follows and requires no further separation. You end the last sentence of a paragraph with a period for the sake of symmetry, and perhaps because you always end every sentence with a period. Omitting something your reader expects to find gains you nothing and may end by confusing him. In an enumeration, you again use the period (or a right parenthesis) as a separator to avoid ambiguity. A number could be misread for quantity and a letter for part of the text. However, a period is usually not used to separate a Roman numeral in a chapter or section heading. There is no possibility of misreading "II Statement of the Problem" for anything else.

Comma

The most widely used separator is the comma. Always bear in mind that this is the only function of the comma: it separates. Omit it if no separation is required or intended. For example, it is customary to separate a string of adjectives from each other. "He is a rude, cantankerous, quarrelsome, self-indulgent, meddlesome old fool" needs the comma separators for emphasis. You want the reader to come to a slight stop and think about every one of the epithets. On the other hand, "old fool" is so close together that you don't want to separate the phrase from its last modifier, "meddlesome," just as you wouldn't use a comma if you left out all the other epithets and simply called him a "meddlesome fool." Adjective and noun belong together; they are never separated; but a string of adjectives must, may, or may not be separated by commas. It depends on the sense and your stylistic preference. "A burly barrel-chested overweight wrestler" could be written as shown without any commas, though most people would prefer seeing commas separating the three adjectives from each other. "Precise, inch-by-inch, second-by-second timing" should have the commas to avoid confusion. It is a matter of preference whether you say "apples, oranges, and pears," or "apples, oranges and pears." The second form is called "open punctuation and is generally preferred in newspapers and other informal types of publications. Writers who prefer the first form claim a greater degree of precision for it. Take your pick.

Modern usage tends to eliminate commas, and sometimes at the expense of clarity. For example, newspapers frequently omit the comma after the introductory clause. "Having stated all his reasons for the reduction in force the chairman proceeded to demonstrate . . ." It's not really ambiguous, but a comma before "the chairman" would make it easier to read the sentence. You would come to a slight pause when reading it aloud, and this pause indicates that you should mark the place with a comma. A practical rule you can follow is to leave the comma out when the introductory clause is less than five words long and put it in if it is longer. But do not apply the rule automatically. Many times you may need the separating comma for emphasis and clarity. "For programmers, the task is simplified . . ." needs the comma if you want to contrast programmers with other types, e.g., mathematicians.

There is really just one golden rule to follow in using commas: Does the sentence read easily and smoothly? Is it clear? Does it convey the intended meaning? A comma may change the meaning, but only your judgment can tell you if it does.

One other rule: If in doubt, leave it out. It is usually better to omit a comma where it belongs than to confuse the reader by placing one where it doesn't. The fallacy of using rigid rules shows up in this sentence culled from a book on American history:

> The judges avoided the confusion of energy that might have hampered them, if they had chosen to defend both the businessman and the negro at the same time.

The author here evidently followed a presumed rule that you always put a comma before "if"; but a comma is a separator, and in this case there should be no separation. The two parts of the sentence that are separated by the comma belong together, and the comma should be omitted.

Semicolon

Next in importance to the period and the comma is the semicolon. For some obscure reason, many people seem to think there is something wrong with semicolons. I don't know where this notion originated or why it should be given currency. The semicolon is a perfectly good punctuation mark that takes its legitimate place halfway between the period and the comma. (Despite its name meaning "half colon," it is never used in place of a colon. This frequent misusage of the semicolon may account for its slatternly reputation.)

As a separator, the semicolon is more emphatic than the comma and less definite than the period. You want your readers to come to a more deliberate pause than they would with a comma. The semicolon is useful in a list of attributes, where readers have to digest each one separately.

> He had enough intelligence to make a careful analysis of the situation; enough foresight to anticipate possible sources of trouble; enough caution to guard himself against unexpected calamities; and enough courage to face the possiblity of disaster.

Commas in this example would be too weak to isolate the separate thoughts; they would not do the job the semicolons do.

A semicolon is also useful in place of "and" and to coordinate two related parts of a sentence.

> Green means "go"; red means "stop."

> In Germany, it rains frequently in August; in November, it rains all the time.

In both examples, a comma would be too weak, a period too strong, and "and" vaguely unsatisfactory. The semicolon can also help you get rid of trailing participles.

> Englishmen are considered unemotional, their public-school upbringing *having trained* them in stoicism.

> Englishmen are considered unemotional; their public-school upbringing *has trained* them in stoicism.

Colon

Period, comma, and semicolon are all stops. The colon has a somewhat different function: it is a mark of emphasis that raises expectations. In Fowler's words, It "delivers the goods that have been invoiced in the preceding words."

> Give me the verdict: Have I passed or failed?

> Make no mistake about it: We believe in rules.

> You have three choices: A, B, or C.

In each of these examples, you raise expectations by "invoicing" something that is to come. A mere comma would be too weak; a period much too final; and a semicolon inadequate and inappropriate. Only a colon will do the proper job of announcing the "delivery" that is about to take place.

With Displayed Listings

The most frequent use of the colon is not within a sentence, however, but at the end of a stem sentence that introduces a "displayed" listing.

> The seven dwarfs had the following characteristics:
> > Goofy was ...
> > Dopey was ...

> XYZ company has branches in 15 states:
> > New York—11 West 42nd Street, New York City
> > California—705 South Spring Street, Los Angeles

In these examples the colon serves as the nail from which you hang your individual items. You should not use a colon if it interrupts the natural flow of your sentence. That is, the colon does not belong after words like include, contain, comprise, consist of, or the verbs to be and to have (is, are, has, have, etc.).

> The three branches of the government are
>> The Legislative Branch
>> The Executive Branch
>> The Judicial Branch
>
> The purchase price includes
>> Spare tire
>> Full tank of gas
>> etc.

In both these examples the listed items could have been written on the same line as the stem sentence without requiring separation by any kind of punctuation mark.

Used sparingly, displayed listings can be effective in drawing attention to things you want readers to remember. The listings may help them scan a text and give them a quick orientation. This is important and you should take advantage of the device. It also breaks up what might otherwise be a solid page of text. This, too, is important. But when you overdo it, giving several displayed listings on every page, then the layout becomes tiresome and the device counterproductive of what you are trying to accomplish. Some lists read better in a straight line than spread out and displayed. Once you give an item the weight of a separate line, you invite the reader to stop and linger. Be sure that the item is important enough to warrant such special attention. Be sure that it has enough relative importance. Emphasis, to be emphasis, must stand out from its background. If you shout all the time, it's the same as if you whispered all the time. Use displayed listings to achieve a change of pace, not as a way of life.

Other problems associated with colons and displayed listings involve capitalization, enumeration, and punctuation.

Do you capitalize the first word after the colon? If it introduces a complete sentence or a displayed listing, yes; if an incomplete, fragmentary sentence, no. This is my own preference and not a rule. Other style guides give different usages. When your listing consists of parts of a continuous sentence, it is generally preferable to start each item in lower case, but only if the item follows an identifier.

> The generator has two functions:
> 1. to recharge the battery, and
> 2. to deliver power to the electrical system.

In the example above, enumeration of the two items is justifiable, barely justifiable. Enumeration is frequently not necessary and can disturb rather than simplify reading. There are usually three good reasons for enumerating: reference identification, hierarchy, and sequence. You may want to refer to a specific item later in the text or possibly while discussing it with someone over the telephone. In either case it will be helpful to refer to the item by its specific identifier rather than by calling it "the third item from the top."

More often enumeration is used to indicate hierarchy. You want to indicate subordination, as in a table of contents. You can achieve much by indenting, but this may become awkward when you end up with an enormous left margin and just a few words of text on the right. A format combining enumeration and indentation is usually best. Enumeration can be by letter or number. A typical scheme is

1.
   a.
      (1)
        (a)
        (b)
      (2)
   b.
2.

Text generally goes back to the left margin in 1. and a., and is blocked under (1) and (a). If your ordering scheme contains more than three subheads under the primary item, you had better take a good look at your structure. Chances are that you may have to restructure your organization for greater clarity, or you may want to drop some of the lower-order listings to avoid confusing your reader with too much detail.

The need for enumeration in listing sequential steps is self-evident. Procedures, for example, require sequence indicators. In technical publications, use of the lowercase letters of the alphabet is standard, with "o" and "l" generally omitted to avoid possible confusion with zero and one.

When there is no need for identifiers, a simple way to make the items of a list stand out is to separate them by proper spacing and identation, and to introduce each item with a "bullet" (●). You should avoid identifiers that serve no specific purpose, because readers instinctively look for the purpose and may become disoriented when they don't find it. Also, unnecessary identifiers are nothing but clutter.

The final problem in displayed lists is punctuation. If your list consists of short items, it is quite permissible to use no punctuation at all. If your list consists of complete sentences, use the same punctuation you would use if the sentence were in the middle of ordinary text. In displayed listings that interconnect from beginning to end, it may be best to use "running" punctuation where you terminate each item with a comma or a semicolon. In mixed lists, use your own judgment.

Can you use a colon after a colon? This question frequently arises in listings. The solution is to convert a second set of colons to dashes:

Vibration tolerance:	Vibration tolerance:
Crated:	Crated—
Uncrated:	Uncrated—

Dash

The dash is underrated as a punctuation device. The German word for dash is *Gedankenstrich*—thought line—a word that conveys the function of the dash. A thought occurs to you and you write it down, introducing it with the dash:

> Management is experienced—perhaps too experienced to be flexible.

A pair of dashes can serve to bracket an incidental notion:

> Freeway traffic—a nightmare during rush hours—presents no problem to the off-hour commuter.

Because of its nervous, spontaneous quality, many writers frown upon the use of the dash in formal publications. I think they're wrong. Anything that makes writing a little livelier should not be suppressed because of its informality. Like any other device, the dash becomes tedious when it's overdone, but it has legitimate uses. It can substitute for a colon; it can introduce a thought, an amplification, or an explanation; or it can take the place of a pair of commas or parentheses for an aside.

Typists frequently use the hyphen in place of the dash, which is the underscore raised half a line. Don't let them do it. The standard form of the dash in a typescript is the double hyphen with no space at either end—like so. In print, however, this mark should always be converted to a proper dash.

Parentheses

Unlike the dash, which is used mainly for emphasis, parentheses should be used for de-emphasis. You put in parentheses information that is incidental to the main line of your thought, indicating to the reader that this information is interesting but not vital.

You can also use a parenthetical sentence in place of a footnote. But you should be wary of using parenthetical qualifiers. They tend to break a reader's stride, forcing him to shift his attention back and forth.

> As a child, Sigmund Freud had ambitions of one day becoming the Austrian prime minister, but a radical change in the political climate soon disillusioned him of any realistic hopes for such a career. (His being Jewish began to matter.)

> A heavy car (over 4,000 pounds) will use more gasoline (regardless of compression ratio) than a lighter car.

In the first example, the parenthetical sentence is a legitimate aside. In the second, the parentheses serve the writer as a crutch for careless writing. With just a little respect for his craft, he would reword the sentence.

> Regardless of compression ratio, a heavy car uses more gas than a light one.

Parentheses have, of course, many other uses, especially in formal writing, where precision and completeness are more important than flow. In the GPO style manual, for example, almost every paragraph contains one or more pairs of parentheses. But the style manual is a reference book, written for discontinuous reading. As a rule, parentheses disturb continuity. Try to leave them out if you want to carry your reader along.

Parentheses are used for explanation and amplification, and occasionally for comment. The commenting clause, though it is also called the parenthetical clause, is generally easier to read when it is bracketed by commas or dashes rather than by actual parentheses.

41 ✍ References, Citations, and Footnotes

The purpose of this chapter is not to duplicate the extensive, detailed coverage in the standard style manuals, but to give a concise summary of accepted practice, with emphasis on the reasons why references, citations, and footnotes are used, and on the situations when they can be omitted.

References

References direct the reader to a figure or table, to another document for comparison, corroboration, or additional details, or to another section of the same document, in which case they are usually called cross-references. Because references tend to be somewhat pedantic and to slow the reader down, they should be used with caution except in scholarly and scientific material where copious references are expected. In an essay or feature article, or any other material directed to the general public, references are usually omitted.

References to tables and figures may be given in parentheses, with or without an introductory "see." Examples: (See Table 7), (Fig. 4). Numbered figures and tables should always be referred to in the text, and the text reference should always closely precede the table or figure, not follow it. References to sources should be given in the notes, where they may be introduced by phrases like "Compare," or "See also," or by "Cf.," which is the abbreviation for the Latin *confer*, meaning "compare."

Cross-references are very popular in all types of instructional material where it is necessary to reassure the reader that something that may bewilder him now will be clarified later, or was explained earlier in a part he may have skipped or forgotten. But as in all writing, you have to exercise judgment not to overdo cross-referencing. Too many cross-references can be as annoying as too few. In giving a cross-reference, make it as precise as possible but try to avoid giving page numbers unless you can be sure that they are not subject to change. The wording that introduces the cross-reference may be terse but should be sufficient for your purpose. For example, "This sequence of events is charted in Fig. 14" is preferable to a bare "(Fig. 14)."

Citations and Footnotes

Citations are a requirement in all scientific or professional writing where the author's research must be validated by citations. Some professions have special ways of citing sources, as for example the legal profession, and some learned journals issue their own style guides instructing authors on how they want citations to be given, but the standard format for citing a book is

1. K. Manning, *Adventures in Disneyland* (2nd ed.*; Los Angeles: Middleground Press, 1972), p. 476.
2. E. Jacobi, *Writing at Work* (Berkeley, Calif.: Ten Speed Press, 1985), p. 188.
3. K. Manning, *op. cit.*, p. 533.
4. *Ibid.*, p. 687.

*First editions need not be identified.

An article in a periodical is cited as

> 5. G. Nimrod, "How to Build a Better Mousetrap," *Gentlemen's Arts*, I(1915), pp. 1–78.

The Roman I refers to the bound volume of the periodical. If the article is referred to a second, third, and fourth time, it would be cited as

> 6. Nimrod, *op. cit.*, p. 67.
> 7. *Loc. cit.*
> 8. *Ibid.*, p. 73.

Loc. cit. refers to exactly the same location as that previously cited.

Although my treatment of citations is sketchy, you'll find it sufficient for your ordinary requirements and less confusing than the detailed explanations in standard reference works.

Some references and all citations are given at the bottom of the page (footnotes), others at the end of the chapter or document. Footnotes are more convenient for the reader, but chapter and document notes offer advantages too: they are much easier to produce and offer the reader the option of reading both text and notes without interruption. For notes may contain much more than just references and citations. They can be used for the writer's comments and for sidelights not directly pertinent to the subject but nevertheless highly interesting and illuminating. At times, notes are the best part of the reading, but in most business communications, notes should be used sparingly. If writers, overflowing with knowledge, information, and enthusiasm, do append notes to their writing, these should not be used for chattiness and point-scoring. Within the context of commercial, financial, and technical publications, only the most factual kinds of notes have any validity.

Reference to notes is made with superscript symbols or Arabic numerals. Symbols are used when numerals could result in confusion, as for instance in a text dealing with mathematics. But symbols become clumsy to use and should be avoided when they need to be doubled, tripled, and quadrupled. Art supply stores sell sheets of small-size transfer numerals that can be rubbed onto the typescript with the tip of a pencil. They will give your note references a distinctive appearance and make them manageable even if you run into three figures.

Footnotes are set off from the body of the text by a horizontal line 1 to 1½ inches long, starting at the left margin. Superscript references are raised one-half line; they are set outside the punctuation mark in the text unless the mark is a semicolon; and they precede without intervening space the first (capitalized) letter of the note itself.

42 ✍️ How to Handle Statistics—Tables and Charts

The main problem with tables and charts is to remember to use them. It is all too easy to get carried away with the flow of narrative prose and end up describing something that should be displayed in a table or chart. Anything that is measured in numbers and units—e.g., 3 minutes, 10 seconds, 50 horsepower, 70 feet—is easier to tabulate than to describe; anything showing measurable changes is easier to plot on a chart than to describe in words. Tables and charts make life easier for both writer and reader. They are to be preferred in all but the simplest cases.

Isolated data can usually be handled within the text, but clusters of data are very difficult for the reader to sort, understand, and assimilate. To use such data for reference is next to impossible. Clusters of data belong in tables and charts.

A table need be nothing more than an indented listing, correlating subjects with data in an informal manner. Such a table need not be identified as a table and will not be referenced in the text other than by its lead-in phrase. It need not have row or column headings. Since informal tables are an integral part of the text, they should not be bulky enough to disrupt the reading pace.

Formal tables are used when

- They cannot be conveniently integrated in the text.
- They require identification by which they can be referred to throughout the text.
- They are sufficiently complex to require separation from the accompanying text.

The first task in setting up a formal table is to determine what the table is supposed to show and what you are going to call it. Frequently the name of the table will be obvious, but when it is not, then the effort to name the table pays dividends. In verbalizing what you are trying to show, you may find that your original concept was too complex or that your idea

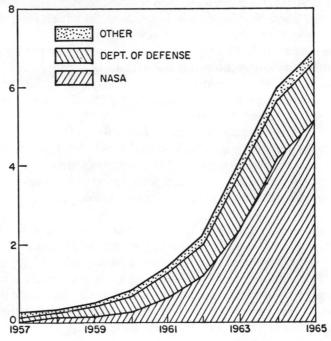

FEDERAL SPACE EXPENDITURES
BILLIONS OF DOLLARS

Federal Space Program Expenditures*

Agency	1957	1960	1965	1966 est.	1967 est.
National Aeronautics and Space Administration	76	329	5,035	5,521	5,211
Department of Defense	48	518	1,592	1,640	1,650
Atomic Energy Commission	19	41	232	201	174
Weather Bureau	—	—	24	19	27
National Science Foundation	7	—	3	4	3
Total	150	888	6,886	7,384	7,064

*In millions of dollars
—represents zero

Fig. 42-1.   Statistical data represented in both graphic and tabulated form.

is unworkable. Giving the table a name will help you clarify things that need clarifying before you can set up the table.

Next you must determine which are your subjects and which your data categories. Again, this is not necessarily obvious. It may depend on your point of view. In a sports statistic your subjects may be the athletes, and the data categories, their performance records; or you may want to look at records and correlate these with the athletes, in which case the records will be the subjects of your table, and the athletes the data.

Since we read from left to right and tables consist of rows and columns, subjects are line headings, placed at the left side of the table, and categories are defined in column headings. Normal reading from left to right will thus give you the subject and all pertinent data associated with it. The "subject" area of the table is called the stub.

Row and column headings must necessarily be brief. Lack of space makes it impossible to be wordy. You must, nevertheless, make an effort to be as fully descriptive as possible. Use footnotes if necessary. Incomplete identification of your categories can lead to extreme reader frustration. Use standard abbreviations throughout the table, both in headings and text.

To help the reader interpret tabulated material, charts are frequently used in support of tables. Charts have the advantage of giving an immediate, visual impression of the changes documented by the tabulated data, sparing readers the effort of making their own interpretations and leading them to the desired conclusion. Examples of statistical data shown in both tabular and chart format are given in Fig. 42–1. Other types of charts and curves are shown in Appendix C.

43 ✍ Description

One of the most important, or at least most frequent, tasks of almost every writer is that of description. The technical writer must describe equipment; the scientific writer, processes and results of discoveries; medical writers, syndromes; political writers, institutions, coalitions, alliances, etc. Description is part of almost every piece of writing, whether it is an essay, a short story, or a technical report.

Descriptions can be boring or interesting, depending on how they are written. A boring description, in general, is one that is purely analytical—passive; an interesting description, one that is functional—active.

An analytical description is one that begins with a listing of the constituent parts of the thing described. For example, "An automobile consists of a chassis, a drive train, a steering and braking system, and a body." Since everybody knows what an automobile is, this description is not particularly jarring, but it isn't particularly informative, either. If you wanted to explain the automobile to someone who's never seen one, this kind of an analytical description would mean very little. The first thing the jungle dweller who has never seen an automobile would want to know is, "What is it for?" He wants to know the function of the thing described. To reach his mind quickly, you have to tell him where, when, how, and under what circumstances the automobile is used. You have to tell him what it does. In short, you have to tell him *what it's for.*

The magic word in any description is the third person, present tense of the verb "to be." The magic word is "is." The automobile *is* a vehicle with a self-contained power source. The dictionary *is* a reference book listing word definitions in alphabetical order. Television *is* a method of electronically recording, transmitting, and reconstituting images.

In most cases you'll find it much more difficult to describe things in terms of what they are than in terms of what they consist of. Giving a breakdown of the constituent parts is the lazy way out. Nobody can fault you for being wrong, even if you are not communicating, and it frequently circumvents the need for sticking your neck out. Describing things in terms of their functions forces you to assume a point of view. You must understand, and your understanding cannot help but reflect your personal philosophy.

Take something as simple as a light switch. You could say, "The mercury light switch is an improvement over conventional switches in that it is noiseless." Or you might say, "A mercury switch is a light switch that costs twice as much as an ordinary switch because it is noiseless." Or a third approach might be, "The mercury switch is safer, longer lasting, more reliable, and in the long run more economical than an ordinary switch because . . ." All three approaches represent different levels of understanding, and different areas of interest. Each in its own way is an improvement over a static description of what the switch consists of and how it works. This will become part of the body of the description, but it should be discussed only after the writer has explained the function of the object, or in this case the function of the change, of the difference, of the improvement.

It is relatively easy to describe an institution or an organization in terms of its parts: its charter, its members, and its administrative set-up. If you start with its charter you will be functional in the sense that you'll describe at least the intended purpose of the organization. You will, in fact, be functional. But few descriptions actually ever begin with the charter for the simple reason that it's usually dry reading, couched in legal language, and permeated with an odor of irrelevance. Nobody takes a charter quite seriously.

Take for example NATO, the North Atlantic Treaty Organization. If you were asked to describe it, you would probably be tempted to start with a listing of the member countries, proceed to a description of its administrative structure, military organization, financial support, weapons procurement, etc. You could write a pretty fair report without ever coming to grips with the functional aspects of the organization. But to make any kind of sense, your report would have to state the purpose of the organization. Why was it formed? What does it seek to achieve? What are the premises for its existence?

In scientific terminology this functional approach is often referred to as teleological. The word comes from the Greek *telos* meaning goal, and *logos* meaning word. Teleological thus means goal-directed interpretation. It is the study of evidence of design in nature. It implies direction and purpose.

Applied to writing, the teleological approach means that "a thing" becomes clearer, becomes understandable, only when we see it in the context of its purpose. Sometimes we have such basic familiarity with the object of a description that, as readers, we supply something the writer has omitted. But careful writers don't take chances on what the reader will or will not supply. They make it their business to state the purpose of the thing described. In other words, their description will be functional.

The scientist investigating phenomena will continually ask himself: What purpose does this serve? He is not satisfied with classifying, cataloging, and reporting. He wants to know *why*. It's the basic question that motivates a person to become a scientist. The writer is similarly motivated by this curiosity about reasons. Playwright Arthur Miller once said that he is interested not in what happens, but why it happens. You can see a similar trend from "what" toward "why" in news reporting in magazines and newspapers. The reason is probably that the immediacy of television reporting has taken the urgency out of the "what" while creating a new urgency for "why." Facts by themselves have never been particularly interesting. They have to be correlated, interpreted, arranged in a pattern that yields meaning. In the terminology of the social scientists, facts have to be "operationalized." In other words, they have to be made functional.

Suppose you have acquired a new sailboat, are thrilled with your acquisition, and want to share your enthusiasm with a friend. You sit down to write a letter. What are you going to tell him? Are you going to give him facts—dimensions, materials, tackle, auxiliary motor, etc.? Possibly, if your friend is also a sailing buff. But you might more reasonably share your enthusiasm by telling him what you expect the boat will do for you, how the features relate to performance: the sails to speed, the hull to maneuverability, the galley to convenience, the deck to parties. Always explain why. If you have redesigned the hull, state why you have done so; what the redesigning will do in terms of speed, durability, safety, or maneuverability. If you've added a sail, explain what its purpose is. There isn't anything that makes much sense except in terms of its design, its purpose. And don't take it for granted that your readers will know. More often than not, they won't. And if they don't, you've lost them.

44 ✍ How to Brag

One of the most difficult but also one of the most necessary writing tasks is that of blowing your own horn without giving offense. Nobody likes a braggart, but unless you brag a little, how do you let people know that you're good? And letting people know that you're good is a constant requirement in most commercial writing. Advertising, of course, is the classic case, but it's only one of many forms of bragging that have to be practiced in the day-to-day intercourse between buyers and sellers, clients and patrons. You'll have to be subtle, to be sure, but you'll have to do a little bragging all the same if you want to get the job, the contract, the assignment, the continuation of funding, or the grant, any one of which is so frequently the objective of your writing effort.

Let's make clear from the beginning what you must *not* do. You must not, ever, under any circumstances, say you are good, not even that you are really good. Even if you're the type who wouldn't be caught dead saying such a thing about yourself, you may still be tempted to say it about your firm, your associates, your team. Mild and modest professional people have been known to become flamboyant promoters when they felt it was necessary for them to be "salesmen." The misunderstanding here lies in a misconception of what selling is all about. It is not bragging. It is not boasting. It is not showing off. It has nothing in common with breathing hard, using oratorical flourishes, and waving the flag of your product or company. The day of the snake-oil promoter conning country bumpkins may not be past, it may never be past, but the style has changed. What was believable yesterday may no longer be believable today, and believability is the crux of all salesmanship.

Self-serving words, even if they're true, tend to detract from the credibility of what you are saying. You may have assembled an "outstanding" team of experts. Don't say it; prove it. The growth curve of your company may be "unprecedented." Bite your tongue. You may have received glowing reports on "the excellence of your performance." Shun the phrase. You may intend to "dedicate all of your energies to the task at hand." Avoid this promise. You may honestly believe that you have achieved "the highest attainable level" of something or other. Resist the temptation of stating it.

Remember the phrase "self-serving words," and test your selling prose by this criterion. Self-serving words are words that carry their own emotional charge, words that require no proof outside themselves, words that permit no argument, words that attempt to glow by the vibrations they presumably set up in the reader. Self-serving words reek of fulsomeness. They're counterproductive.

The trick in bragging without giving the appearance of patting yourself on the back is to be factual. Objectify your achievements. One of the greatest sales pitches ever written was David Ogilvie's famous ad, "At 60 miles an hour the loudest noise in this new Rolls-Royce comes from the electric clock." The ad then goes on to list 19 points that prove that the Rolls-Royce is the best automobile in the world.

In writing promotional material for yourself or your company, you can achieve the same effect by being factual: citing actual growth figures; showing graphically the rising curve of sales and profits; listing awards and citations; enumerating contracts on which you have performed; and underscoring the features of your product.

Most people will do this automatically and well. The difficulty arises when you try to summarize all the good things you have done. Here the temptation to use a self-serving value statement becomes almost irresistible. It seems so legitimate to call something good when you supply ample proof later on that it *is* good. Maybe it is, but don't forget that there will be a physical separation between the proof and the self-serving value judgment and that the casual reader may never get as far as the proof. You will be safer being factual even in your summaries. It takes a little thought but it can be done, in most cases quite easily, by using quantities and percentages. For example, instead of boasting of your outstanding team of experts, you can cite the aggregate years of experience, the number of advanced degrees, numbers of patents held and papers published, honors and awards received, etc. To show your project management capability you may want to cite just one example, making reference to an appendix or another section where other examples are given.

Bragging is a difficult art, and it becomes doubly difficult when you have little to brag about, which is when you're usually most in need of it. It goes to the essence of salesmanship and resists simple formulations. You must be believable, and to be believable you must at least give the appearance of sincerity. A show of modesty can be valuable as long as you give the appearance of being better than you claim to be, but any appearance of weakness and self-doubt can be fatal.

So go ahead and brag. But be aware that it's an art requiring thought, skill, and an enormous amount of tact.

---

45 Writing the Press Release

Although press releases are usually written by professional PR people, the ability to write one can be useful even to the occasional writer. Publicity is an important tool for furthering one's interests, and the press release is one way of getting it.

A press release serves to announce some kind of news for publication in a newspaper or trade magazine. It is written to obtain publicity for its subject matter, to draw favorable attention to a certain facet of the news it presents, or to prevent adverse publicity by giving its own version of the news. The press release is always and unashamedly self-serving.

Editors are swamped with press releases. They use them knowing they are self-serving, and use them gladly if the release contains valid news of interest to their readers. Editors simply don't have the manpower to cover every facet of their field, and they depend on press releases for at least part of their news coverage. They'll be grateful for a release containing accurate and informative news reporting. They may even print inaccurate and slanted news—once. Don't burn editors by misleading them if you plan to place a story with them more than once.

In rare cases an editor will print publicity in exchange for advertising. A good example is the real estate section of most metropolitan newspapers, where much of the "news" consists of publicity releases submitted by advertisers. Even here, however, it is wise not to abuse the courtesy; give the release the appearance of valid, interesting, and accurate news.

In writing your release, stick closely to the format of the standard, non-bylined newspaper story in being factual and complete. Avoid editorial comment. Give the most important part of the news in the first paragraph and add details in subsequent paragraphs. Then if the editor has to cut your story, he can snip away from the end while preserving the essentials.

If possible, give at least one direct quote by an authoritative spokesman who may be considered the actual source of the story. This enhances the authenticity of the news item and makes the presentation more lively.

Editors love pictures, so try to enclose a photograph if there is any aspect of your story that can be photographed. Keep in mind that pictures and stories may become separated, and that the picture alone may be printed and not the story. Therefore, attach the picture caption to the picture and let the caption speak for itself, without reference or need of reference to the story.

With respect to format, remember these guide lines:

1. Identify yourself. Make it clear who is the source of the release and who can be contacted for further information.
2. State the date on which your story may be printed. Since editors cannot print your release on short notice, you must send it a few days before the event you wish to publicize. Editors respect release dates and will not print your story before the specified date.
3. If your release is for exclusive use by a certain publication, make sure to state so at the top of the release: FOR RELEASE EXCLUSIVELY BY . . . : date. Some papers will not print a general release.
4. Put a date line at the beginning of the first paragraph (e.g., Washington, June 16—) unless the release is for local news media only. The date should be the date of the event, not the date of writing, or that of anticipated release.
5. If the release date is immaterial, state "FOR IMMEDIATE RELEASE" in your top line. In this case be sure that your release does not reach the papers before the date given in your date line.
6. Do not write a headline. You don't know where and how the story will appear and must leave this to the discretion of the editor and the makeup man. A one-line identification of the subject matter may be helpful, however.
7. Use 8½ × 11 bond, preferably white; double-space all copy; do not use carbon copies; use wide margins; avoid hyphenating words at the end of a line; do not carry paragraphs over from one page to another; staple two or more pages together and number the pages if more than two; indicate the end of your release by three number signs (# # #).
8. Photos should be 8 × 10, glossy. Give caption on a flap at the bottom of the picture.
9. If your release is about an individual, identify him or her as completely as possible. "Mr." is usually omitted, but "Mrs., Miss, or Ms." is for some reason not omitted. If your subject is an award-winning scientist or a championship amateur golfer, by all means say so.

Your release should cover the six points news stories usually cover: who, what, where, when, why, and how. All six points are important, but be careful not to let them clutter your story and particularly your lead

MAYOR TOM BRADLEY

Contact: Bob Kholos   485-5182

Date: TUESDAY, MAY 14, 1974

Release: IMMEDIATELY

ERNST JACOBI, coordinator on Mayor Bradley's staff for all projects

... the handicapped, is on "social service" leave from Xerox

FROM: Los Angeles County Epilepsy Society   CONTACT: Flora Baer or Betty J. Ticho
2911 West 8th Street
Los Angeles, CA 90005
(382-7337)
FOR IMMEDIATE RELEASE

NEW SERVICES AVAILABLE FOR EPILEPSY PATIENTS

The Los Angeles County Epilepsy Society (LACES) has begun a project to inform substantially handicapped epileptic persons in the county of new services available to them under the Developmental Disabilities Services Act.

This project is funded by a state grant aimed at "encouraging the maximum use of Regional Centers' facilities by unserved, substantially handicapped epileptic children and adults."

These new benefits for epileptics have become available through recently enacted legislation, explained Mrs. Betty J. Ticho, executive director of the Epilepsy Society (LACES); and they may run the gamut from diagnosis to occupational therapy, day care, activity programs and many more areas of need.

"To qualify for services at one of the seven Regional Centers in Los Angeles County, epileptic persons must be developmentally disabled as well as substantially handicapped," said Mrs. Ticho. "A person is regarded as developmentally disabled if his disability began prior to the age of 18."

Individuals subject to epileptic seizures, or the parents or guardians of such individuals, are asked to call LACES (382-7337) for information about possible qualification for Regional Center services. Those thought eligible will then be referred to the Regional Center closest to them.

#########

Fig. 45-1.   News releases.

sentence. You must use judgment and let yourself be guided by your sense of proportion in deciding on the amount of detail you want to supply under each head. You must determine what is important and what is not. For example, if your company is releasing a new product, what is more important, the product itself or C. Charles Hasenpfeffer, President, who is making the announcement? Policy may not always give you a choice in the matter, but it will serve you well to keep the principle in mind. Figure 45-1 shows two typical press releases.

46 ✍ Résumés

Anyone looking for a job needs a résumé. Though a résumé will not by itself get you the job, it is the necessary first step for being considered. Thus it is worth whatever effort it takes to write a good one.

A résumé serves to list your accomplishments and display your experience. Its style should be crisp, terse, and elliptical, leaving out all personal pronouns and clutter words. You're under no obligation to mention failures, make excuses, or in any way apologize for yourself. Without padding, make the most of your triumphs. Without exaggerating, stress the importance of the work you've done and the positions you've held. If you are applying for a specific job, stress your most applicable experience. If you've received honors and awards, make a point of them. If you hold patents, list them by name and number. If you've published papers, give titles and publication data. State your professional associations. Don't leave out anything that can enhance your status. Your résumé is not the place for showing modesty or diffidence.

The format shown in Fig. 46-1 reflects my own preference but is by no means the only acceptable one. If you prefer another, or find one more suitable for your specific qualifications, don't hesitate to use it, or to modify the one shown. But do remember these points:

1. Give the résumé visual appeal. It is your calling card. It should not be a glossy, expensive production job that makes you look like a professional job hunter. It should look (and sound) sober, factual, and businesslike. It should be neat, clean, well-typed, and free of typographical errors and misspellings, and it should be well laid out. It is nice

to get it all on one page, but it is better to use several pages than to overcrowd one. Always bear in mind that you are in a competitive situation or you wouldn't submit a résumé at all. Make its appearance count.

2. Make the résumé easy to read and scan. Yours will not be the only résumé to come to your prospective employer's desk. Present your information in a crisp, spare, uncluttered style. Avoid wordiness. Lead your reader to what you want him to know about you.

A personal résumé should cover all of the areas covered in the sample format (Fig. 46-1). The circled numbers refer to these comments:

1. Some people prefer the word "résumé" here. In my opinion this is unnecessary.
2. *Personal Data.* Many people include social security number, date and place of birth, health, and appearance in this block of data. Also, they like to preface this information by the appropriate categorical headings (e.g., marital status: married). Again, I find this superfluous, causing clutter without serving a useful purpose.
3. *Age.* Use your judgment on whether or not to state your age. I would not if overaged or underaccomplished, or both.
4. *Education.* Skip high school diploma if you have a college degree. List advanced degrees in ascending order as shown: B.A. first, M.A. next, Ph.D. last. Keep institutional details to a minimum. That is, Harvard University is enough. Cambridge, Mass., is unnecessary. Don't list grade average, but do mention honors. If your academic qualifications are less impressive than your experience, feel free to move this category to the bottom of your résumé. Many people prefer it there anyhow.
5. *Objective.* Unless you plan to send a cover letter stating your objective in specific terms, it is a good idea to indicate the kind of job you want. The buckshot approach—you want a job, any kind of job—isn't much appreciated by prospective employers. They're looking for someone who fits a specific opening, and if your objective fits in with their requirements, you're past the first hurdle. Don't be afraid of pigeonholing yourself. You can keep your objective broad enough to give yourself some leeway while making it specific enough to indicate your interests and aptitudes.
6. *Summary of Experience.* This is precisely what it says it is: a concise statement of your professional, vocational, business, or managerial experience—a thumbnail sketch of your achievements and capabilities. It should be phrased so that it will support your stated objectives.
7. *Detailed History.* This accounting of your working years is the meat of your résumé. You might preface this section with the word "HISTORY:" but I don't think this is necessary. Note listing of dates in reverse order, that is, last or current job first, first job last. Give month and year of start and end of employment. Try to maintain

RICHARD JAMES
17850 Spruce Lane
Middletown, Calif. 91000
(213) 727-3440

① ③ ②
28, married, no children
"Secret" clearance
U.S. citizen
Will relocate

EDUCATION: ④
Stanford University, BSEE (cum laude), 1964
University of California, Los Angeles, MBA, 1968

OBJECTIVE: ⑤
Project management with full responsibility for time,
cost, and technical performance.

SUMMARY OF ⑥
EXPERIENCE:
Seven years, analysis, design, and development of
advanced systems, last three with management responsibility. Proposal writing. Ship-to-shore telecommuni-
cations; automatic fare collection; inertial guidance
—analog, digital, and hybrid systems.

July 1970 ⑦
to present
⑨
Litton Ship Systems, Culver City, Calif. ⑧
Associate Project Manager, Ship-to-Shore Telecommuni-
cations, Advanced Design Destroyer (ADD) Project.
Report to Director, Communications Design and Development, Ship Systems Division. Participated in original
proposal effort and continued to project completion.
Achieved all goals for time, cost, and technical
performance.

•
•
•

June 1964
to May 1966
⑨
Teledyne Systems, Inc., Hawthorne, Calif. ⑧
Project Engineer, Instrument Section, Assault
Helicopter Alignment (AHA) Project. Participated in
design of accelerometer-computer interface. Performed
systems analysis and received recognition (President's
Award) for a comparative analysis of different types
of accelerometers that significantly influenced the
final design. Did . . .

PUBLICATIONS:
"Economics of Automatic Fare Collection Systems," Bus
and Rail, II, p. 879 (1969), Aneurin Godiva, coauthor.
•
•
•
"Digitizing Accelerometer Outputs," Coordinates, VII,
p. 225 (1965).

PATENT: ⑩
Wishbone Accelerometer, #759030046 (August 1967).

AFFILIATIONS:
IEEE, American Management Association.

HONORS AND
AWARDS:
Four-year member, California Scholarship Society;
National Merit Scholarship; Dean's list, three years;
Phi Beta Kappa.
President's Award, Outstanding Contribution, Fourth
Quarter 1965.

Fig. 46-1.   Personal résumé.

continuity of dates, accounting for discontinuities if you can. (On the other hand, there is no point in accounting for periods of unemployment.)

8. *Employer Identification.* Give name and location of employer with enough detail to allow complete identification, but not so much as to clutter your résumé. In other words, street address, zip code, telephone number, company department or section are not desirable.

9. *Description of Experience.* This is the most difficult part of your résumé to write. Observe these points:

- Give exact job titles. Use separate paragraphs and separate job titles for successive jobs held with the same employer. *Example:* SENIOR TECHNICAL WRITER. Wrote and edited a variety of technical manuals . . . .
  TECHNICAL WRITER. Prepared user and design manuals

- Indicate department or section, task or responsibility. *Stress responsibilities.* Don't give the name of the person you reported to, but do give his or her title. E.g., "Reported directly to Vice President, Marketing . . . . " Be specific about what you did and accomplished. *Examples:*
  "Developed a simplified filing system that provided faster document retrieval while cutting filing time in half."
  "Initiated computerization of spare parts provisioning system that resulted in a 30 percent reduction of inventory."
  Note the elliptical, telegraphic style, with all personal pronouns left out.

10. *Miscellaneous Data.* This block of data is self-explanatory and mentioned only to complete the checklist. State the following:
    Publications
    Patents
    Honors and Awards
    Committees
    Affiliations

Standard format for résumés is letter size (8½ × 11), typed on white bond of good quality and reproduced on a clean machine. Blueprint or thermofax copies are not desirable.

Do not include in your résumé:

- Salary information—if necessary, this can be handled in a cover letter.
- Photograph of yourself, unless one is requested.
- References. There is no reason why anybody should call your references until after they have talked to you, at which time you can submit a list of names.

Conciseness is much to be desired. The average résumé should not be over two pages long, and none should exceed four pages. The last ten years are the period of significant experience. Anything previous can be dropped or summarized.

47 ✍️ Indexing

To be fully useful documents of more than 25,000 words require an index. A good index leads the reader quickly and easily to specific items of interest, not leaving him "hung up" because the word or phrase he's looking for isn't listed, or the page he's referred to doesn't show the word or phrase he looked up but deals only with a related concept. A poor index is frequently cited as the major weakness of books that critics otherwise admire.

One reason why so many books suffer from this neglect is that indexing cannot be done until the book is paginated—months after the author had his last contact with it; he may by that time be deeply involved in a new project and want only to be done with the old. Besides, indexing is difficult and tedious work under the best of circumstances. Much indexing is done by professionals who are specialists in the field, but the average author can't afford them and has to do the job himself. It's bad enough to do the proofing of the galleys; adding an index at this stage looms like sheer torture.

Computer-aided indexing, while it cannot eliminate the decision-making function of the indexer, can at least lighten the burden of manual indexing. The standard method of indexing is to read the entire document word for word, select key words and phrases, write these on 3 × 5 file cards, make cross-references as necessary, sort the cards into alphabetical order, consolidate multiple entries on a single card, and then type this card file in alphabetical sequence in the desired index format.

Selecting key words and phrases of potential interest to the reader is a job that cannot—and should not—be delegated to an automated procedure. Ideally, it should be done by the author, who knows best what is significant and what is not. Most authors do not find the job of selecting and eliminating objectionable. What they do find objectionable, because it is time-consuming and unrewarding, is the manual labor involved in the mechanics of indexing—preparing, shuffling, consolidating, and eventually listing hundreds of file cards. These tasks can now be accomplished with much less effort, with greater speed, and with more accuracy by a computer with a sort (i.e. alphabetizing) program. Make a first pass through the final, paginated copy of the document and underline each name, word, or phrase you want to include in the index. On a second pass, enter each item plus page number into the computer. Then instruct the computer to sort the entries and edit the alphabetized list either directly on a video terminal or on the print-out.

Editing the alphabetized listing is simple: Redundant entries are crossed out and their page numbers added to the first-occurring entry; or they are consolidated so that only modifications are listed below the initial entry. A nice refinement, particularly in textbooks and reference documents, is to list the most significant entry first, letting all others follow in order of occurrence.

To summarize, letting the computer do all the time-consuming clerical tasks takes the tedium out of the indexing job and allows the indexer to concentrate on the things that are important in building a useful index:

- Selecting key words and phrases of interest to the reader
- Cross-referencing
- Deciding which of several entries is the most important and should be listed first
- Selecting subentries to be listed indented below principal entries

Developing a useful index requires a good deal of thought and work even with the aid of a computer, but this cost is negligible compared to the improvement in usefulness of a properly indexed book.

48 ✍ *Producing Your Document*

Assuming you have proofed, error-free copy laid out in a pleasing format, the method of reproducing your document will depend on the number and type of people you want to read it, and the impression you want to make on them. A memo intended for only a few readers can be duplicated on a copying machine, but a report or proposal intended for wider circulation requires some thought. Although in most organizations production will be handled by a professional, it will be useful for you to know something about the field, if only to enable you to plan and make informed decisions about the final appearance of your document.

Typed or Typeset?

Typewriters and word processors both produce typed copy. Word processors give you more format control, but their output is (for best quality) still produced by a printer similar to a typewriter. Typesetting has its advantages: It looks better, saves space, and gives you a much wider choice of type fonts (sizes and styles). Disadvantages are that it costs more and may take longer. These disadvantages weigh lightly, though, when measured against the appearance of the final copy. Typesetting should be used for brochures, pamphlets, stockholder reports, catalog sheets—any publication produced in quantity and intended to have more than passing significance.

Offset or Duplicate Printing?

The difference between offset printers and high-speed duplicators is that offset printers require a plate whereas duplicators print directly from the original. Despite the high quality that can now be achieved with duplicate printers, offset printers are still preferable for some publications.

Offset printing is more expensive, but the difference becomes insignificant on large runs, and should definitely be disregarded when "tone art" (photographs, paintings) is to be reproduced. Also, duplicators cannot easily reproduce nonstandard formats. Generally, once you go to the expense of having copy typeset, you should have it printed on an offset press.

Size Reductions

Tables, charts, and drawings are frequently done on pages much larger than the standard 8½ × 11 inch page on which they are reproduced. They must be reduced in size before they can be printed. Most copiers let you reduce the original to various sizes. The offset camera, on the other hand, gives you complete control over what portion of the material you want to reduce, and by how much you want to reduce it.

If you want to print only a portion of a photograph or drawing, you don't have to cut your picture. You can instruct the printer to print only the desired portion by placing "crop marks" on the border of your image. (Pasting the picture on an "illustration board" makes this easier.) You can also use crop marks to indicate the desired reduction. Figure 48-1 shows the two types of crop marks.

As shown, you need to specify only the reduction for the larger dimension. The camera automatically reduces the other dimension proportionally. For example, if you have a drawing 24 inches wide and 30 inches long, and your reproduction image area is 6 × 7 inches, you simply specify 7 inches alongside the 30-inch side of the original. If you want to know the amount of reduction for the other dimension, you can calculate this with simple arithmetic:

$$\frac{\text{old length}}{\text{new length}} = \frac{\text{old width}}{\text{new width}}$$

Substitute

$$\frac{30}{7} = \frac{24}{X}$$

and you get

$$X = \frac{7 \times 24}{30} = \frac{168}{30} = 5.6 \text{ or approximately 5⅝ inches.}$$

An inexpensive tool called a "sizing wheel" is available to do these calculations for you so that you can read them off as you would on a slide rule. In addition, the sizing wheel gives you the reduction/enlargement percentage, which is the data the printer uses to set the camera.

If material is to be enlarged instead of reduced, a simple graphic method of sizing is to draw a diagonal across the original and extend it to where it intersects with one of the lines framing the available image area. Drawing a line across the open side of the frame, either at the top or at the right-hand side, completes the format enlargement. This method can, of course, also be used in reverse for determining a reduced dimension.

Writers should also be aware of what is meant by "portrait" and "landscape" layouts. Portrait, or vertical, layout has the narrower dimension at the bottom, and landscape, or horizontal, layout has the narrower dimension at the side. Landscape figures and tables often have the advantage of fitting more naturally on the page, using space more economically and requiring less reduction. The disadvantage is that the reader has to twist the book to view the material and read the caption. With landscape layout, captions and titles are conventionally along the longer dimension, at the top for a table and at the bottom for a figure. The top is nearest the binding edge on a right-hand page, nearest the outside on a left-hand page.

Photographs

If they show what you want them to show, photographs are the best of all possible illustrations. Photographs can be improved by (1) airbrushing, (2) adding callouts, (3) eliminating clutter, and (4) cropping.

Airbrushing. A good airbrush artist can do wonders with a mediocre, murky photograph by cleaning it up, eliminating shadows, and restoring details that were previously invisible. The airbrush artist can even mend or straighten parts that are broken or twisted on the original. Be aware, however, that airbrushing is slow and painstaking work performed by highly trained and skilled artists. It is expensive.

Callouts. An arrow drawn on a photograph may become invisible in the darker portions of the photograph. Self-adhesive arrows on a white background are available at any art supply store.

Eliminating clutter. Frequently a piece of equipment is photographed in a cluttered laboratory showing a confusing and messy background. The printer can eliminate this background and other extraneous material through various techniques, for instance by painting it out on the negative with opaque paint. You indicate to the printer on an overlay what you want done, and he will then "drop out" the background and print the photographed object by itself without any background. This also has the advantage of eliminating the gray screen through which the photograph is shot.

Cropping. As discussed above, images should be cropped to show only those portions of interest to the reader. All others should normally be eliminated.

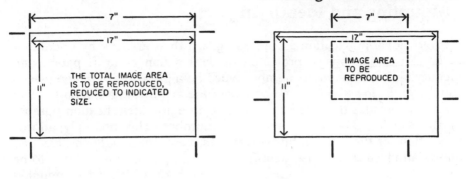

Fig. 48–1. Crop marks.

Renderings

Renderings are produced, often at considerable cost, to create an illusion and stimulate the imagination. A good airbrush artist can take an engineer's concept and make it look like an existing piece of machinery. Other types of renderings are done in oil, acrylic, crayon, or water color. Although these lack the photographic appearance of airbrush work, they can still be a powerful enhancement of a presentation that might otherwise lack sparkle. All these types of renderings would be reproduced as halftones. Considering that they represent a considerable investment, they should be reproduced with the greatest of care.

Handling Art

The most widely used, because it is the least expensive, way to present art to the printer is to paste it on the repro pages and let him shoot it in place. With line art, you use photostats, reduced from the original size to final size (or intermediate size if the entire repro master page is oversize and needs to be reduced); with halftones, you use same-size velox prints made from the halftone negative. If you are short of time and help, you may have to go to the extra expense of getting line negatives and metal plates, and letting the printer strip in your art as indicated on the repro masters. Either way, you will have to know how to indicate desired reductions (or enlargements) and how to crop an illustration so that only a desired portion will be reproduced. You should also know how to mount your artwork. This protects it against damage from handling and enables you to file it for future use.

Mounting and Identifying Art

Professional publication groups safeguard their artwork by bonding it to an illustration board, protecting it with a flap of kraft paper, and identifying it with a unique number typed on a piece of Avery and placed usually in the lower right-hand corner of the art. Information on the flap normally includes the figure number and title, the identification number of the artwork, and the printer's job number. This not only affords protection for the artwork but also makes it easy to handle and file, and allows an illustration to be identified from the printed page if it is to be reused for another job. The illustration board on which art is mounted also provides space for placing crop marks and indicating sizing.

Scheduling

When you are working against a deadline, you'll frequently come up against emergencies. Most of these you'll be able to control by increasing your effort: working around the clock and hiring additional help, notably typists and illustrators. Two elements, however, are beyond your control—transit, time for your document to reach its destination, and turnaround, time from sending your job to the printer to getting it back. Some printers are set up to handle a job overnight, even between midnight and 8 a.m., but you had better not rely on it unless you've checked with your printer first. Also, he may be able to do it one time but not the next because of a rush job from another customer who got there first. If you're on a tight schedule, you'll find it advisable to make arrangements well in advance, with back-up arrangements if the job is large and important.

Printing and Binding Instructions

It is important to know what instructions to send along with your package to the printer. He must know whether to print on one side of the page or both sides, what pages to leave blank, and whether to collate and bind the job. Most important of all, if your illustrations are not integrated with the text copy, he needs a list of illustrations. And you want to be very sure that you have clearly identified both the illustrations and the corresponding places where they go in the finished job.

Your instructions to the printer can be quite informal, but they should be clear. On a document that is to be produced "saddlestitched" (stapled in the center), you would be well advised to make a paper dummy showing clearly what goes where. Saddlestitched documents are usually produced in units of four pages ("signatures"); to be on the safe side, make sure that your page count, including blank pages, is a multiple of four, or check with the printer about signature size. When documents are printed on both sides of the page, the odd-numbered page is *always* a right-hand page. Although the page numbering will be a clue to the printer, to avoid mistakes it is always best to indicate pages that are to be left blank.

Besides instructions indicating proper page sequence, you have to give your printer instructions on

- Paper stock (color and weight; 50# offset is standard weight)
- Cover stock
- Collating
- Stapling (side stapling or corner stapling, if any)
- Saddlestitching (if applicable)
- Drilling (three holes or two holes; 5/16" diameter must be specified, if desired)
- Color of ink (black is standard)
- Trimming (8⁷/₁₆" × 10⁷/₈" is often preferred to 8¹/₂" × 11")
- Binding (see below).

Binding

You may find it helpful to know what types of binders are available for your proposal or report. The most common type of binder for short reports or papers is the plastic spine with transparent plastic covers between which the pages are inserted into the spine. The major disadvantage of this binder is its impermanence. Pages can easily be pulled out, or they may even slip out accidentally. Also, anything that is much over ¹/₈-inch thick will not easily fit into the spine.

Comb-binding is probably the most widely used method for binding reports and proposals produced in limited editions. A comb is a plastic spine with 19 circular prongs that are threaded through matching holes in the paper. Simple hole-punching and threading machines are available, and the combs come in a wide range of colors and sizes. The threading is done by means of a gadget that spreads the comb open. The same gadget is used to disassemble an assembled book in order to change, insert, or remove pages. With this type of binding, pages cannot be lost accidentally or be removed without a degree of deliberation. The combs, 19-hole paper punch, and comb spreader are manufactured by General Binding Co. Practically all printers have them and will use them to comb-bind your book if so instructed.

Perfect-binding is a method that glues the back edge of a sheaf of paper flat to the spine of the cover, which may be of any material but is generally of paper. Paperback books are bound by this method. The major disadvantage of this binding is its very permanence: You can't change any pages without tearing the book apart. Another disadvantage is that normally you can't do this binding "in house," but have to send it to a printer. However, a table-top machine for perfect-binding is now available.

"Velo-binding" is an inexpensive, permanent-type of binding. Instead of gluing the edge of the book to a cover, Velo-binding uses two narrow strips of plastic (one with prongs, the other without) and fuses them under pressure through holes punched at the edge of the paper. The result is a remarkably strong binding edge that allows a book to be opened almost flat. (This, incidentally, is a major advantage of comb-binding—that the comb allows a book to be opened completely flat for easy readability.) The Velo-Bind machine is a compact, table-top machine that takes hardly more space than an office typewriter.

Appendices

APPENDIX A
Proofreading Guide

Marginal Mark	Textual Mark	Meaning
incident /	The isolated went unnoticed.	Insert marginal entry where indicated by caret.
ℓ	The extra letters was removed.	Delete or take out.
ℰ	The extra s pace was removed.	Delete and close up.
stet as set	The ~~hurts~~ injured child was hospitalized.	Let it stand as originally set/ typed.
#	Hesupplied the correct version.	Insert space.
ˆ	John Pat's brother, came to the table.	Insert comma.
;	He approached the gate he entered the courtyard.	Insert semicolon.
⊙	Find the following formula weight and equivalent weight.	Insert colon.
⊙	The filter was removed	Insert period.
(set) ?	What did you say	Insert question mark.

Marginal Mark	Textual Mark	Meaning
!	He said: "Wow" ∧	Insert exclamation point.
∨'	Mikes pad was missing.	Insert apostrophe or single quotation mark.
∨	R_2x	Insert prime.
❝ / ❞	∨Africa in ∨was Perspective the book reviewed.	Insert double quotation marks.
=/	John is a long∧ distance runner.	Insert hyphen.
(/)	5∧y+x∧	Insert parens.
[/]	5(y+x)½ ∧ ∧	Insert brackets.
¶	∧In Sec. 1-5, the theorem and proof of congruency were presented.	Paragraph; start new paragraph.
no ¶	In Sec. 1-5, the theorem and proof of congruency were presented.⊃ ⊂Also shown....	No paragraph; run in to preceding line.
run in	x = 4+y²⊃ ⊂= 81	Run in (on) material on same line.
run over	The committeeman showed his displeasure over the motion.	Carry over to next line.
run back	The drawn line was une#⊃ ⊂ven.	Carry back to preceding line.
∫	x²+y²+z²∫= 5a²+6	Mark off or break; start new line.
] or ⌐	To align the top] line, move it to the right.	Move to the right.
[or ⌐	[To align the top line, move it to the left.	Move to the left.
][or ctr	]5a²[x² + y	Center.
⊓	He ran the 440 in record time.	Move up.
⊔	He ran the 440 in record time.	Move down.

Marginal Mark	Textual Mark	Meaning
=	The chairman con-vened the meeting.	Straighten type; align horizontally.
‖	The chairman convened the meeting.	Align vertically.
tr	Set in captials.	Transpose.
lc	Africa in Perspec-tive.	Set lowercase letter.
cap or ☰	The scope dis-played the ir loss.	Set in capitals.
sc or ☰	The schematic had and and or gates.	Set in small capitals.
ital	Africa in Perspec-tive.	Set in italics.
rom	Africa in Perspec-tive.	Set in roman.
bf	Africa in Perspec-tive.	Set in boldface.
lf	**Africa in Perspec-tive.**	Set in lightface.
wf	The storm inter-fered with the reception.	Wrong font; reset in correct type.
cap & lc	voltage output or voltage output	Set in lowercase with initial capitals.
∨²	$x_2 + y^2 = 1$	Set as superscript.
∧	$x_1{}^2 + y = 1$	Set as subscript.
⊗	correction	Broken letter.

APPENDIX **B**

Inductive/Deductive Writing

Compare the underscored portions on the left with their placement in the rewrite. These key sentences were moved from the bottom of the paragraph to the top. The resulting change of focus then required other changes to avoid redundancies and wordiness. Since "1.0" and "1.1" were the only two heads in the entire paper, they served no useful purpose and could be removed.

1.0 INTRODUCTION

For an effective contract definition effort on the Rapid Loading/Unloading Ship, a number of associated sciences must be reviewed. This review requires study of present methods for accomplishing the steps towards fulfillment of the RLUS mission. One such attendant technology involves the study of cargo loading and unloading from the RLU ships. Technical studies are underway on established methods for performing this task. These studies have exposed characteristic rates and fundamental principles which associate with these methods. The compromises suggested by this preliminary information indicate that at least one combination of methods is worthy of consideration. This <u>method employs a floating landing stage for handling barges, lighters and</u>

FLOATING LANDING STAGE FOR RAPID LOADING/UNLOADING SHIP

A technical review of established methods of loading and unloading cargo has suggested a compromise <u>method employing a floating landing stage for handling barges, lighters, and other cargo carriers.</u> The preliminary engineering calculations presented here are intended only to show feasibility and should not be construed as the results of detailed design.

<u>The flotation concept combines the favorable characteristics associated with large containers and continuous action.</u> The highest handling rates are achieved by methods that move cargo in large loads. That is, systems using large containers tend to be faster than systems using small ones. Illus-

other cargo carriers. This paper describes the more basic specification requirements and operating procedures associated with the method. The preliminary engineering calculations are intended only to show feasibility and should not be construed as the results of detailed design.

1.1 LOADING/UNLOADING SYSTEM CHARACTERISTICS

Our review of the many methods of loading and unloading has shown certain fundamental tendencies. The methods which have demonstrated the highest handling rates (tons per hour) have been systems which move cargo in large loads. For example, one of the very highest rates was achieved by railroad cars coupled together and pulled off as a train.

Systems that employ large containers have tended to be faster than systems that employ smaller containers. Disconnecting the rail cars and removing the individual cars resulted in lost time. This same tendency appears in other methods of handling in that "continuous" systems show more favorable rates than "interrupted" or discontinuous systems. Another example of this is the major loss of unloading rates when forklifts have to compete for the availability of a single loading port instead of entering one and leaving in tandem by another.

The flotation concept described here combines the apparently favorable characteristics of employing large containers and providing for continuous action.

trating the concept of continuous action, one of the highest rates of unloading has been achieved when railroad cars were coupled and pulled off as a train. Disconnecting the cars and pulling them off individually obviously results in lost time. Another example of the advantage of continuous versus "interrupted", or discontinuous, systems is the major degradation in inloading rates when forklifts have to compete for the availability of a single port instead of entering one and leaving by another.

APPENDIX C
Charts and Graphs

Some excellent books on chart making are available to those who want to go into the subject in detail (see Appendix E). This appendix offers an overview; it introduces some basic techniques and briefly explains and displays the types of charts that are most commonly used. The charts shown are almost entirely from the *Pocket Data Book, USA 1973*, produced by the Bureau of the Census and published by the U.S. Government Printing Office, Washington, D.C.

Milestone Charts

The milestone chart is the most basic and perhaps the most useful of all charts used in commercial communications. It depicts schedules and schedule histories by showing scheduled events (goals) on a time scale. The standard symbol used for a goal, or milestone, is the delta (Δ), filled in to indicate completion, or preceded by a number (#Δ) to indicate the nth time an event has been rescheduled. Slippage of a milestone date, as distinct from a rescheduled event, is generally indicated by a square turned 45 degrees (◇), again blank for projected slippage and filled in (◆) for a slipped and completed (but not rescheduled) event. "Time now" lines and arrows serve as graphic indicators showing actual completions and slippages. For greater graphic clarity, the lines between the start of an activity and its projected finish should be heavily shaded to the left of the time-now line. To avoid clutter, comment and identification should be given at the bottom of the chart, keyed by callouts. Fig. C–1 is an example of a milestone chart shown in two parts reflecting two stages. The first stage (top) is the initial schedule projection. The second stage (bottom) shows schedule status at approximately three-fourths projected completion. As a result of unanticipated delays in obtaining clearances and approvals, slippages have occurred and some goals had to be rescheduled.

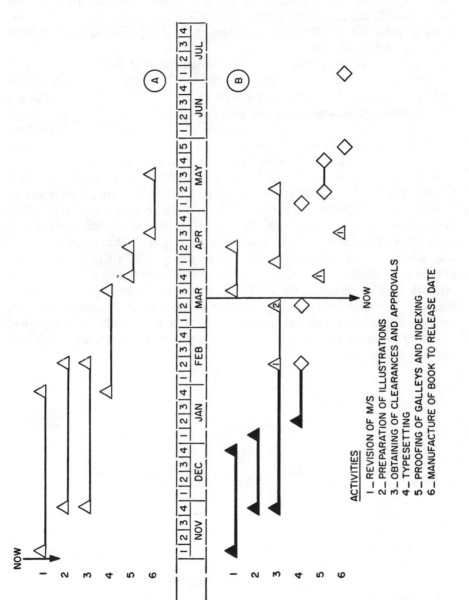

Fig. C-1. Milestone charts at start (A) and at projected 3/4 completion time (B).

Network Charts

Proposal writers and managers blanch at the very mention of the word "network." It conjures up visions of PERT charts stretching around the walls of lofts filled with drafting tables—an anticipation known to have caused severe headaches.

PERT is an acronym for Program Evaluation and Review Technique. It was introduced as a management tool by the Navy in the early 1960s and proved successful in tracking and reducing cost overruns and slippages of large and complex procurement projects. But PERT requires specialists for implementation and is an unworkable tool for the individual writer. What is not unworkable, however, and can be useful for the lone writer/manager is a PERT chart called the "Critical Path" network.

A critical path network can be constructed for even simple projects having a limited number of elements. It forces the project manager to analyze the work to be accomplished, isolate discrete elements (activities), determine which can be accomplished in parallel and independently of each other, which are predicated on the completion of what other activities, and which, therefore, is the critical path along which the project must proceed. It shows the manager where slack exists and minimizes the possibility of a portion of the available work force being idled and stalled because one critical element has not been completed. As a communications tool, the critical path network serves to inform every member of the project of his or her role and responsibility in relation to everybody else's role and responsibility.

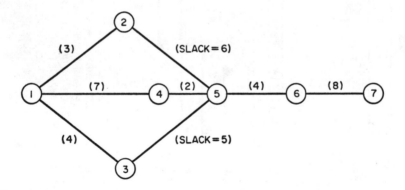

Fig. C–2.   Critical path network.

Fig. C–2 is a simple network consisting of only six activities. The work units required to accomplish the tasks associated with each activity are indicated in parentheses. It can be seen that activities 1–2, 1–3, 1–4, and 4–5 must all be completed before activity 5–6 can begin. It can also be seen that activity 1–2 can be started up to six, and activity 1–3 up to five work units later than activity 1–4 because of the indicated slack.

Obviously this simple network analysis will have an impact on the development of the milestone chart, show the manager the most economical way to use the available work force, and serve as a communications tool for everybody involved in the project.

Flowcharts

The literature tends to neglect flowcharts, dismissing this important analytical tool with one or two examples that usually lack the modern flowchart's most important element: the decision block. Flowcharting has become a necessity in computer programming, since the computer's ability to "branch" to alternative program paths on the basis of "decisions" is the principle on which programming is based. Analyzing and explicating a process in the format of a computer program flowchart is a fairly recent development that should be used whenever a process or procedure involves two or more alternative approaches.

Fig. C–3 is a flowchart that illustrates the decision-making process involved in acquiring a home. The "entry" point is labeled "Transfer," the assumption being that a transfer from one area of the country to another is the catalyst that starts the process. The three alternatives are to build, buy, or rent. Since this flowchart analyzes the "build" path, "rent" and "buy" are shown as "exit" points which, in turn, become "entry" points on their own flowcharts. Entry and exit points are conventionally shown inside the "race track" used here. The "connectors" labeled A, B, and C are useful devices for keeping the diagram from getting cluttered and unreadable. Connectors are used when you have to continue the flowchart to another page, or to an insert on the same page, or to another part of the chart on the same page to avoid crossing, or using an excessive number of lines. The diamond shape of the decision block is also conventional.

Column Charts

Column charts are used for showing discrete quantities in discrete periods, e.g., dollars per month, tons per quarter, number of shares traded per day, gallons per hour, etc. The "independent variable," measured along the horizontal axis (abscissa), is almost always a unit of time. The "dependent variable," expressed by the height of the column, i.e., measured along the vertical axis (ordinate), can be anything that can be measured and expressed as a quantity—dollars, tons, carloads. The column chart conveys at a glance what statistics convey only through intellectual interpretation: comparison—period-to-period comparison of measured quantities.

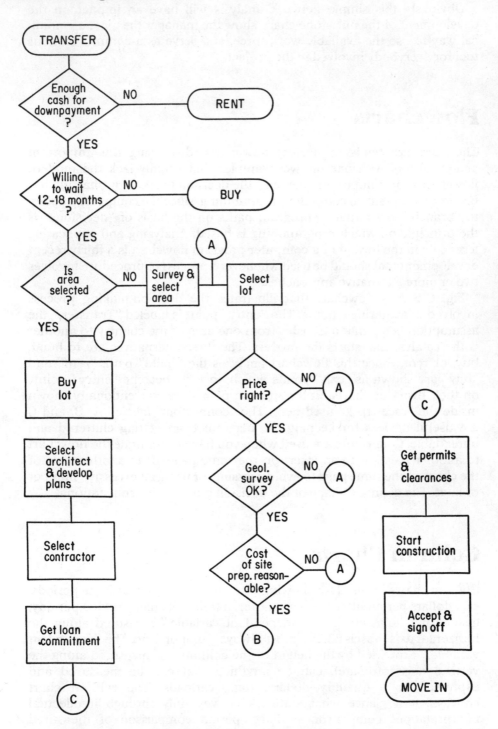

Fig. C–3.   A typical flowcart.

Columns can be grouped to display changes in related quantities, and individual columns can be segmented to show the composition as well as the changes, or the resistance to change, of the composition of each column total. A typical column chart is shown in Fig. C–4. To avoid distortion—frequently unfair and self-serving—columns should always start at zero base line.

Bar Charts

The number of bar charts in the *Pocket Data Book* is almost the same as that of all of the other charts in the book combined. Bar charts are ideal for comparing large numbers of different categories—the meat of census data—whereas other types of charts are oriented more toward representing value versus time for single, or at least relatively few, categories.

Bar charts differ from column charts in that the values to be displayed and compared are plotted horizontally instead of vertically. The decision on which type to use hinges on which is easier to draw in the available space, which is less cluttered and hence more pleasing to the eye. Since the standard page is higher than it is wide, it follows that the vertical axis is usually the longer one. For example, to compare the populations of the world's 20 largest cities, it is obviously easier to list the names of the cities in a column at the left than try to squeeze them side by side along the horizontal axis. Thus, your material will usually dictate the type of chart to use—column or bar. Fig. C–5 shows a typical bar chart.

Line Charts

Unlike the column and bar charts, which show discrete totals, line charts show continuity and thus convey a greater sense of movement and rhythm than do bar charts. In business reports, line charts are used typically to show cumulative values such as units delivered or dollars expended, usually with a separate plotted line showing projected totals for comparison with actual totals, and also a "time now" line or arrow to fix the point in time for which the chart is current. (See Fig. C–6.) A solid line is conventionally used for actual values, and a broken or dotted line for projected and anticipated values.

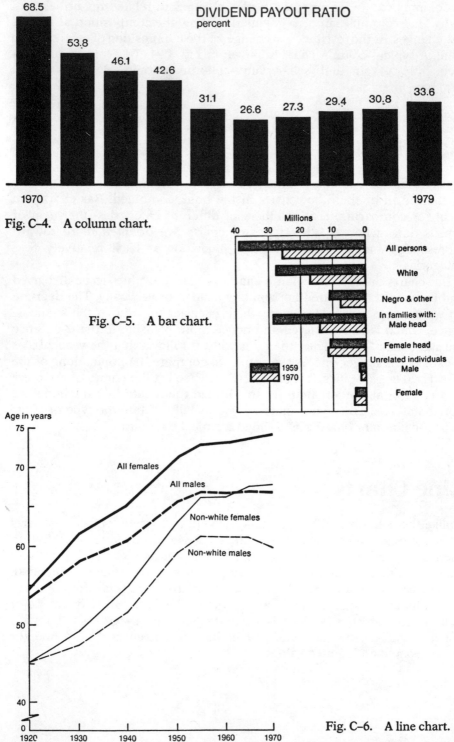

DIVIDEND PAYOUT RATIO
percent

68.5 53.8 46.1 42.6 31.1 26.6 27.3 29.4 30.8 33.6

1970   1979

Fig. C–4.   A column chart.

Millions
40   30   20   10   0

All persons
White
Negro & other
In families with:
Male head
Female head
Unrelated individuals
Male
Female

1959
1970

Fig. C–5.   A bar chart.

Age in years

75
70
60
50
40
0

All females
All males
Non-white females
Non-white males

1920   1930   1940   1950   1960   1970

Fig. C–6.   A line chart.

Band Charts

Band charts are somewhat similar to line charts, except that the area below the topmost line, which represents the total, is subdivided into bands, or strata, each representing a subtotal. As can be seen from Fig. C–7, a band-chart representation of related values makes for a very effective comparison.

Pie Charts

Pie charts are generally considered the easiest to read of all types of charts. They are limited, however, to showing percentages of the whole. A typical pie chart is shown in Fig. C–8.

Rate Charts

Rate charts, also called ratio charts, are used to compare the rate of change of two or more grossly unequal quantities. For example, to make a graphic comparison of the fluctuations in stock A, ranging from 254 to 150, and stock B, ranging from 29 to 13, would be totally misleading if the two price movements were to be plotted on an arithmetic (i.e., evenly divided) scale. The decline in the A curve would appear much steeper than the almost flat curve of the B plot. To make a realistic graphic comparison it would be necessary to use a logarithmic scale where the divisions, as on a slide rule, get smaller as the value gets larger.

Fig. C–9 illustrates the process of how the rate scale eliminates distortion by using semi-logarithmic graph paper for plotting curves representing unequal magnitudes. The paper can be obtained from any stationery or engineering supply store, and plotting the data requires no conversion of any kind. The reason for *semi*-logarithmic paper is that the logarithmic scale is necessary only along the vertical axis, not along the horizontal one, which usually represents time.

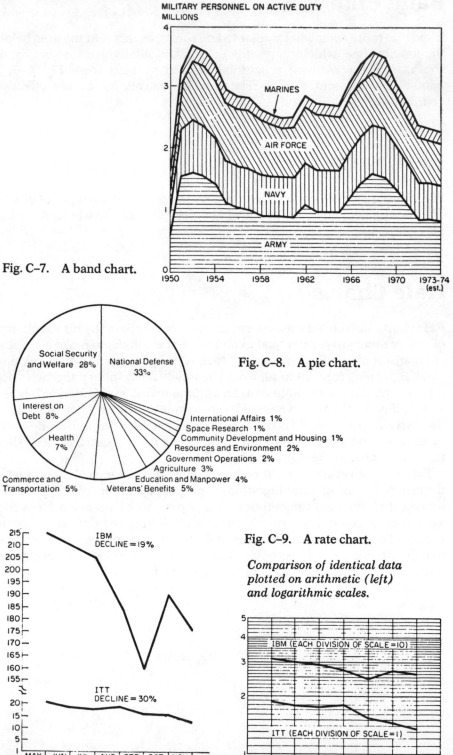

MILITARY PERSONNEL ON ACTIVE DUTY
MILLIONS

MARINES

AIR FORCE

NAVY

ARMY

1950   1954   1958   1962   1966   1970   1973-74
(est.)

Fig. C–7.   A band chart.

Social Security
and Welfare 28%   National Defense
                          33%

Interest on
Debt 8%
                              International Affairs 1%
                              Space Research 1%
Health   Community Development and Housing 1%
7%   Resources and Environment 2%
                              Government Operations 2%
                              Agriculture 3%
Commerce and   Education and Manpower 4%
Transportation 5%   Veterans' Benefits 5%

Fig. C–8.   A pie chart.

215
210   IBM
205   DECLINE = 19%
200
195
190
185
180
175
170
165
160
155

20   ITT
15   DECLINE = 30%
10
5
1   MAY   JUN   JUL   AUG   SEP   OCT   NOV

Fig. C–9.   A rate chart.

*Comparison of identical data
plotted on arithmetic (left)
and logarithmic scales.*

5
4
          IBM (EACH DIVISION OF SCALE = 10)
3

2
          ITT (EACH DIVISION OF SCALE = 1)

1   MAY   JUN   JUL   AUG   SEP   OCT   NOV

APPENDIX D
Exercises

I hope that this book has steered you in the right direction, told you what to do and what not to do, given you advice on strategies, informed you of available tools and techniques, and given you reassurance that you're not lost in the wilderness when confronted with a writing task at work. Now you must put your knowledge to the test by actually writing. As with any other skill, you need practice to perfect your writing skill, and the only way to do this is to stretch your writing muscles and write.

The exercises and the workshop project in this appendix are captioned by chapter numbers, challenging you to apply what you've learned in a given chapter to a task or situation requiring those skills. Don't skip these exercises. Unless you exercise your knowledge by applying it to practical tasks, you'll find that it will quickly evaporate. As you do these exercises, your theoretical knowledge will become tangible achievement. The skills you acquire by doing them will never totally desert you.

Chapter 1

You guessed it! Write a letter to a friend about any subject that engrosses you or is otherwise dear to your heart. If you can think of nothing better, write to your friend explaining why you bought this book and are reading it. But there must be other facets of yourself and your work you may want your friend to know about. When you're finished, you might even put the exercise in an envelope and mail it. Both you and your friend may find the experience enjoyable.

Chapter 2

Analyze any piece of writing, using the guidelines given in Chapter 2, to determine why it did, or did not, hold your interest. Write a brief critique, either of the chapter or the piece you analyzed.

Chapters 3 and 4

Find one or more examples of writing addressed to a "captive" readership. Determine in what way the writer failed to "face the reader" and assume the "communicative attitude."

Chapter 5

Go back to the letter you wrote as an exercise for Chapter 1. Does it have something to say? If it does, write a brief defense against a presumed attack; if it does not, be your own critic and determine where you went wrong.

Chapter 6

1. Write a paragraph or two stressing positive aspects of your profession or occupation. Write it so as to counter and deflate commonly held misconceptions.
2. Write a letter to Benjamin Franklin, describing to him the modern phenomenon of the automobile. Be careful to avoid confronting Ben with unexplained words and concepts with which he cannot be familiar.

Chapter 7

1. Write an essay about a significant event of your past. Take the first event that comes to mind—it is usually the most significant. Point up the event's significance by showing its effect on the present, i.e., by using perspective.
2. You've had an interview for an important job. At the end, your prospective employer asks you to write him an autobiographical essay beginning with the words, "The most significant fact about me is ..." Write it.

Chapter 8

Working quickly and spontaneously, write down lead sentences and short lead paragraphs on as many topics as you can think of. Also try your hand at the lead-ins of obituaries of prominent people who recently died. You'll find that, more often than not, you'll come up with a philosophical statement that indicates the theme you instinctively wish to adopt.

Chapters 9 and 10

Write one or more introductory paragraphs on a subject that interests you, incorporating the principles explained in the last two chapters. The relevancy of your subject to your reader may be obvious from the nature of the problem—or the point may have to be made more specific. Think about it.

Chapter 12

1. Rewrite the following "inductive" paragraphs to make them more forceful and to the point by giving them a "deductive" organization:

    a. We have now terminated our research effort to investigate the advertising claims of six different brands of cosmetics for men. Brands A, B, E, and F (see Appendix I for brand identification) claim that their preparation prevents dehydration of skin due to exposure to wind and sun. Brands C and D make the claim that they supply special nutrients to the skin that will preserve its natural moisture and flexibility far beyond its natural span of youthfulness. All brands guarantee that their daily use will result in no "undesirable" after- or side-effects and will maintain the skin in "glowing health." Our research was conducted on a group of 24 men aged 35 to 55 years. These were subdivided into six groups of four men each, matched with respect to age and complexion, two for each brand and two serving as controls. Skin moisture and flexibility tests were given to all subjects at the beginning of the test period and at regular weekly intervals thereafter. Our test results show that no significant differences could be detected in the skin condition of any of the 24 test subjects before, during, or at the termination of the test period.

    b. Over the last three years we have been engaged in extensive research having for its objective the development of prosthetic and orthotic devices using new materials and techniques that are now becoming available as part of the "fallout" from our aerospace programs. We are presently under contract to the U.S. Veterans Administration to develop an artificial knee joint made of graphite and are experiencing some difficulties in machining and molding this material at an economically feasible cost. We have also conducted limited investigations into the feasibility of using titanium alloys but have not, at this point of time, progressed to any attempt at casting and molding this material.

Because of the preliminary nature of our investigations and as yet limited experience with, and exposure to, these relatively new-technology materials, we feel that we cannot at the present time offer a sufficiently strong capability to successfully achieve your stated objectives of obtaining a capsule hatch hinge within the range of the indicated specifications and capable of withstanding the specified degrees of stress, strain, and temperatures. Accordingly we must regretfully decline to give an affirmative response to your referenced Request for Proposal.

c. Air Force Systems Command Manual AFSCM 5-1, entitled "Publications Management: Technical Documentary Reports," requires that, in the briefest manner consistent with clarity, the abstract of a report will summarize the purpose of the work described in the report, the course of action followed, the results obtained, and the conclusions reached, as applicable. In a classified TDR, the abstract will be assigned a security classification strictly according to the content of the abstract alone. The statement "This abstract is Unclassified," "This abstract is classified Confidential," or "This abstract is classified Secret," as applicable, will appear above the abstract. It should be noted, however, that if the abstract must be classified, AFSCM 5-1 states that "special effort will be concentrated on eliminating classified information for the version (of the abstract) to be used on the catalog card." It is the opinion of this office that the abstract appearing on the catalog cards of the final report for Contract AF 33(603)-3712 is unnecessarily classified Confidential, and could be downgraded to unclassified by the removal of all references to the operational Mach number capability of the subject equipment. Accordingly, this is to request that the recommended change be accomplished, and substitute unclassified catalog cards be prepared and supplied to this office by not later than 23 November.

2. You have an assignment to write a report for your company's house organ or some other similar publication on some person in your organization. Dig up an anecdote about your subject and use it for the opening paragraph. Write only this paragraph and the beginning of the next to show the direction you are taking in exploiting the anecdote's significance. To simplify the exercise you may wish to substitute someone, or something, you know extremely well—your brother, husband, wife, sister, roommate, dog, cat, automobile, lawnmower, television set—and write your anecdote about that.

Chapter 13

1. Select a report or proposal topic that appeals to you. (See "Workshop Exercises and Projects," below.) Then write an outline that will persuade your instructor, your boss, or the editor of a targeted publication that the angle you have adopted is an effective one. For example, if you selected the fund-raising proposal you might summarize the reasons why you believe your firm is in a good position to win the contract and outline the fund-raising methods you wish to propose.
2. You've talked the project over, have agreed on certain changes and details, and been given the go-ahead. Now write a "responsive" outline that will set forth the points agreed upon, further details, and the line of argument to be adopted.
3. Write a checklist of points and topics you have to cover, order these into a system of major heads, minor heads, and subheads, and write a categorical outline where each of the items fits into its proper category.

Chapters 15, 16, and 43

1. Write a description filled with loving detail of something that gives you pleasure. The "something" can be something you now own—a new stereo set, a sailboat, a motorcycle—or it may be something intangible for which you have real love and understanding, e.g., the game of football or Beethoven's late quartets. The point of the exercise is that you write a description, and do so with understanding and enthusiasm.
2. Describe your favorite hobby or pastime, giving as much detail as possible. The emphasis in this exercise is on something you do, and why you like doing it, whereas in the previous exercise it was on an object.
3. Describe an everyday object you like and use frequently, e.g., a pencil sharpener, can opener, typewriter, vacuum cleaner. Give sketch and dimensions if necessary to clarify description.
4. Describe a recent, or soon-to-be-made, acquisition (house, automobile, refrigerator, TV set, etc.) and stress the reasons you chose *it* in preference to some other competing *it*.
5. Write a step-by-step procedure for performing some thoroughly familiar routine. Examples: Changing an automobile tire, changing a typewriter ribbon, preparing a meal, repotting a plant, getting up in the morning and going to work, getting yourself ready for work or school, performing a specific job function.

6.   Your organization has an opening for a job similar to your own. At your employer's request, you are to write a letter to an acquaintance, currently employed, describing the job and persuading him or her to apply for it. You are expected to send a copy of your letter to your employer.

Chapter 36

The following six exercises are all "difficult" letters, because they depend for their effectiveness not so much on content or form as on that almost indefinable quality: tone.

1.   Harry Frobisher, merchandise manager of Broadhurst's department store, has given Formfit Sweaters, Inc., a large amount of business over the years, but Formfit is unhappy because Frobisher is taking advantage by arbitrarily returning unsold merchandise for credit without a shred of justification. These returns are cutting deep into the profitability of Formfit's business with Broadhurst's, but for a number of reasons Formfit would, on balance, rather continue doing business with Broadhurst's and absorb the returns than lose the account and get the payments settled. Write a letter, assuming you are the president of Formfit, persuading Frobisher to adopt a fairer attitude, settle the disputed balance of the account, and remain a customer at the same time. Bear in mind that Frobisher is hardboiled, ruthless, and aware of his power, but that you, as an independent business man, have to retain your self-respect if you want to continue being successful.

2.   At your employer's request, you persuaded an acquaintance to apply for a specific job opening with your organization. Your acquaintance has been interviewed for the job and been found wanting. You are asked to write and break the news to him. Good luck!

3.   You have received an attractive job offer in another city but are undecided whether to take it because (a) you are not anxious to move and (b) your boss is in Europe and won't be back for another couple of weeks; you don't want to quit while he is away and do want to give him the opportunity to match the offer. The people offering the new job are in a hurry and want you to decide quickly. Write them a letter that will keep your options open.

4.   You have been designated by your organization to head the annual drive on behalf of spastic children, a charity of special interest to the head of your organization. At a cocktail party some months ago you met and talked briefly with Tom Halliburton, the general manager of the city's most influential radio station. You would like to enlist that man's help in getting publicity for the drive, especially since the man in charge of public-service broadcasting has been quite

uncooperative in previous years. Write a letter to Halliburton, knowing that he probably won't remember you personally, though he will no doubt recall the party at which you met him.

5. A respected and influential acquaintance, Dr. James Hobbema, has personally asked you to participate in a sociological survey he is conducting. This will involve personal interviews, conducted by his staff, and filling out several long questionnaires. Although you have been assured of complete confidentiality, you are skeptical of the security arrangements but would not want to admit that this is your primary reason for not wishing to participate. Write a letter to Dr. Hobbema, declining with thanks.

6. Mr. Warner Benson has written the following letter to the president of your city's bus company:

> Dear Sir: This is a complaint. I am furious and I want to see action. I am blind; I depend on the bus to get to and from work, and on the bus driver to give me a modicum of assistance. During this past week, the driver of No. 59, whose name I don't know, has three times—three times!—neglected to tell me when my stop came up. I can't see for myself, so I depend on the driver. When I finally got off three stops later, I had to cross the street in heavy traffic and wait for a bus to take me back. I wouldn't care so much if this were just a mistake. But it happened three times in one week. I know that man does it to spite me. I have asked him to call out my stop. Why doesn't he do it! My ears are good. I would have heard him, even sitting in the back. There is no excuse for treating a blind person as this driver is treating me. I will not tolerate it. I want this man to be disciplined. I want you to make an example of him.
>
> Yours truly,

You work for the bus company. You get the job to reply.

Chapter 37

Almost everybody, whether in business or a profession, in civil service or still in school, has some kind of a project in mind that needs to be developed into a report or proposal. This would be the best workshop exercise. But if no such natural topic presents itself, you can pick one or several from the suggested report and proposal topics that follow.

Report Topics

1. Recently at a large party you delivered yourself of some rather harsh criticism of the organization you are associated with. Afterwards a

quiet, middle-aged gentleman walked up to you, introduced himself, handed you his card, and stated, "I'd like you to report this to me in writing." The gentleman was, of course, the head of your organization, whom you had never met. You're stuck with your opinions. Now write the report. You evidently made some valid points or the boss wouldn't have asked for them in writing.

2.   Your local elected representative has asked for your opinion, as an actual or potential consumer of services, on the state of public transportation in your area. Describe the existing system as it appears to you, its problems, and suggested solutions.

3.   Write a critique of the school system in your state and locality. Write only about those aspects with which you are familiar, whether as a parent, relative, student, teacher, or administrator.

4.   Alternatively, write a report on any other subject that interests you and about which you are knowledgeable.

5.   Write a report on the vacation policy in effect at the business or institution you are associated with. If you are not employed, describe the vacation benefits you would like to receive if you were employed. Be sure to answer questions such as: How much vacation entitlement should there be after what length of service? Can unused vacation time be accrued, and if so, how much? Does employee have a choice whether to take cash or time off? Can vacation time be lost if not taken? Who schedules vacations? What is the policy regarding legal holidays when they occur during, or at either end of, the vacation period? When sick leave runs out, can the employee substitute unused vacation time? Can vacation time be taken during lay-offs? How are leaves of absence counted toward length of service? Can vacation time be used in conjunction with, or instead of, leaves of absence?

6.   Write a memorandum to your boss describing your job: both what it is and what you think it ought to be, or what you'd want it to be.

7.   Somewhere in your daily routine there is doubtless a snarl that you'd like to see straightened. In a memorandum to the person with authority to take the necessary action, describe the problem and suggest a solution.

8.   Where do you hope to be ten years from now? Write a report on your personal and career goals, i.e., where you want to go and how you expect to get there.

Proposal Topics

1.   McCullum Eldridge, your city's wealthiest son, has left it a legacy amounting to an annual income of about ten million dollars for the specific purpose of beautifying the city. Another stipulation is that the funds are not to be used for ongoing maintenance but only for new, one-time, tangible projects. The city fathers have decided to hold an

annual proposal competition: All projects from all offerors will be considered provided the budget calls for expenditures of not less than $500,000 and not more than $5 million. The request for proposal (RFP) is brief and to the point: State the problem, describe your solution, explain how you will carry it out, identify yourself, and tell us how you are going to run the project and account for the funding.

2. You are the manager of a prominent fund-raising firm, competing with other fund raisers and public relations firms for the account of the National Foundation for the Preservation of Our National Resources, which wishes to raise funds to support these goals:

   - A public relations program to awaken the public's consciousness
   - to the threat to our natural resources posed by industry, resort
   - operators, and a careless public.
   - Advertising in support of the PR program.
   - Lawsuits to enjoin offenders.
   - Research.
   - Emergency purchases of threatened areas.
   - Lobbying for favorable, and against unfavorable, legislation.
   - Miscellaneous.

The fee will be a fixed percentage of the gross take, not subject to competitive bidding. Write your proposal.

3. You are associated with a modeling school and also do volunteer work with delinquent girls, helping them to become rehabilitated. You feel that at least part of the girls' problem is the low opinion they have of themselves, which you believe would improve dramatically if they were to learn and practice better personal grooming and achieve greater poise. Your idea is to have professionals in the field, teachers from your modeling school, provide this training for these girls under a grant from your state's Department of Rehabilitation. Write the narrative portion of your proposal, describing the training program as you envisage it.

4. Under your city's charter, the Harbor Department is obligated to have an outside firm conduct a survey at least once every ten years to make an inventory of the department's property and facilities, analyze its operations, and evaluate its efficiency. The department is large, employing about 3,000 people, covering a vast area, and owning millions of dollars' worth of sophisticated equipment. It also has a large data processing installation. The department's request for proposals is advertised in the city's metropolitan newspapers, inviting interested parties to send for the RFP. Consider yourself the head of an engineering or accounting firm capable of undertaking such a survey, and write a proposal in response to the RFP. Bear in mind that you will be in competition with many other offerors, hence your approach, methodology, and capabilities will have to be more outstanding than those of your competitors to win the award.

Chapter 45

1. The head of your organization has been appointed a member of an important presidential commission. (Make one up to fit his or her specific interests and capabilities, e.g., President's Commission on Equal Rights for Women, P.C. for the Employment of the Handicapped, P.C. for the Adoption of Metric Measurements by the Apparel Industry.) Write a press release announcing the appointment, for use by trade or professional publications and the local newspaper.

2. Write a release on behalf of a local real estate developer, to be printed in the Sunday real estate section of your metropolitan newspaper. The event to be publicized is the opening of the first model home of what is to be an 80-home development. Give your imagination free rein on location, design features, price, terms, and availability.

3. Write a release on the progress of a local charity fund-raising project in which a member of your organization plays a prominent role. Although the local paper has been generous in giving coverage to this project, not much that's newsworthy has been happening lately, with the drive at about the half-way mark. Think of some kind of a news angle that will give the paper an incentive to print your release.

APPENDIX E

My Personal Bookshelf

Although I've never been an avid collector of specialized books on writing, I've managed over the years to accumulate a modest but useful collection of such books almost in spite of myself.

Books on Language and Usage

The first book I acquired, and one I still use from time to time, is *Plain Words: Their ABC*, by Sir Ernest Gowers.[1] It is concise, witty, and easy to read and understand, and has a useful index. The same author became the editor of the 1956 edition of *Fowler's Modern English Usage*,[2] a classic of its kind, famous for its good common sense as well as its hectoring style. Not always a model of clarity, it is frequently entertaining and always useful when you try to make up your mind about certain locutions. Serving a similar purpose, easier to use, but less sprightly, are Theodore Bernstein's *The Careful Writer*[3] and Rudolf Flesch's *A Guide to Plain English: The ABC of Style*,[4] a handy book available in paperback. My favorite among this type of book, though, is a fairly recent addition, William Safire's *On Language*.[5] As a speech writer for former Vice President Spiro Agnew, Safire was credited, or discredited, for Agnew's famous alliterative put-down of critics as "nattering nabobs of negativism." Though I'm rarely

---

[1]New York: Alfred A. Knopf, 1957.

[2]H. W. Fowler, *A Dictionary of Modern English Usage*, 2nd ed., revised and edited by Sir Ernest Gowers (New York and Oxford: Oxford University Press, 1965; and New York: Atheneum, 1965).

[3]New York: Atheneum. 1965.

[4]New York: Harper and Row, 1964.

[5]New York: Times Books, 1980.

in agreement with Safire on politics, I admire him as a writer and language "maven" (expert), as he sometimes refers to himself. I always read his weekly essay on language in the *New York Times Magazine*, and enjoy reading his book culled from these essays. Rather than clothing himself in a mantle of authority, Safire deals with dilemmas and presents differing points of view. His essays are invariably lively, and his language glitters. Not infrequently I finish reading one of his essays with a belly laugh, or at least a chuckle.

Enjoyable, too, though not particularly useful as reference books, are Edwin Newman's *Strictly Speaking*[6] and Bernstein's *Watch Your Language*.[7] Both useful *and* enjoyable is a slim volume by David Ogilvie titled *Confessions of an Advertising Man*.[8] An advertising tycoon famous for some brillantly successful campaigns, Ogilvie knows, and shares, a great deal about the art of persuasion.

Advice on Writing

Among the books giving advice on writing, the most elegant and useful is, to my mind, that old standby, *The Elements of Style*, by William Strunk, Jr., and E. B. White.[9] E. B. White is one of my literary heroes. His collected *Essays*,[10] though not specifically on writing, are a treasure trove for all who are interested in language, both as an art and as a craft. The *Elements* consists of only 78 pages of text, but these few pages contain the essence of writing wisdom. Rudolf Flesch, too, has written a thoughtful book of essays, titled *How to Write, Speak and Think More Effectively*.[11] The essays are interesting and instructive, each making a point with respect to one or another aspect of communication. Finally, no list of essays would be complete without a mention of George Orwell's "Politics and the English Language,"[12] which should be required reading at least once a year for all who make a living, directly or indirectly, by setting words down on paper.

[6]Indianapolis, Ind.: Bobbs-Merrill, 1974.

[7]Great Neck, N.Y.: Channel Press, 1958.

[8]New York: Dell, 1963.

[9]New York: Macmillan, 1972 (2nd ed.).

[10]New York: Harper and Row, 1977.

[11]New York: Harper and Row, 1963.

[12]In *A Collection of Essays by George Orwell* (New York: Harcourt Brace Jovanovich, 1970).

Reference Books

Among reference books, one that is never out of my reach is the dictionary. Over the years I've accumulated four, one *Webster's Unabridged*, two different editions of *Webster's Collegiate Dictionary*, and the *American Heritage Dictionary*,[13] which I like best for everyday use because it has lots of pictures. I like pictures. The *Style Manual* published by the Government Printing Office is a book I use regularly for resolving questions on form, compounding, hyphenation, etc. For more complex editing tasks, I generally refer to *A Manual of Style* published by the University of Chicago Press. I also own *Roget's Thesaurus*,[14] which I use about once a year, and three books of quotations, *Bartlett's*,[15] *A New Dictionary of Unusual Quotations*,[16] and *Humorous Quotations*,[17] which I have disciplined myself to use sparingly. Finally, the *Harbrace College Handbook*[18] is a useful reference on grammar, mechanics, punctuation, and other topics.

Among books on printing and production I especially recommend an inexpensive paperback, the *Pocket Pal*,[19] subtitled *A Graphic Arts Production Handbook*, which is precisely what it is—information on printing methods, paper, copy preparation, typesetting, art preparation, and many other topics. Another book, *Print and Promotion Handbook*,[20] has also been useful to me over the years. A third, *Words into Type*,[21] is considered all but indispensable by professionals in book publishing.

Grant Proposals

For people writing grant proposals, an invaluable reference is Virginia White's *Grants*.[22] The book is a sure-footed guide through the labyrinth of foundations and government agencies willing to hand out money to those who know how to push the right buttons.

[13]Boston: Houghton-Mifflin, 1978.

[14]*Roget's International Thesaurus* (New York: Crowell, 1977).

[15]*Bartlett's Familiar Quotations* (Boston: Little, Brown, 1968).

[16]New York: Alfred A. Knopf, 1952.

[17]*The Dictionary of Humorous Quotations*, Evan Esar, Editor (New York: Doubleday, 1949).

[18]New York: Harcourt Brace Jovanovich, 1982 (9th ed.).

[19]New York: International Paper Co., 1974.

[20]D. Melcher and N. Larrick, 2nd ed. (New York: McGraw-Hill, 1966).

[21]Marjorie E. Skillin, 3rd ed., (Englewood Cliffs, N.J.: Prentice-Hall, 1974).

[22]New York: Plenum Press, 1975.

Charts and Graphs

The only book on charts and graphs that I own is Darrell Huff's *How to Lie with Statistics*,[23] a witty, tongue-in-cheek guide to statistical misrepresentation. Among the books on the subject that I know, I consider the *Handbook of Graphic Presentation*[24] the most instructive and useful. Eleanor Spear's *Practical Charting Techniques*[25] is an exhaustive treatise containing approximately 250 example charts, and Tom Cardamone's *Chart and Graph Preparation Skills*[26] delivers what the title promises—a nuts-and-bolts approach to chart-making. Also, chapters on charts and graphs are contained in most textbooks on business and technical writing. Fast becoming the most common method of generating graphs and charts, however, is to use the computer. The only program I'm familiar with is Supercalc3,[27] an electronic spreadsheet that lets you develop graphs as well as column and bar charts.

Textbooks

For what it's worth, these are the textbooks I've used in my own classes: *Shurter's Communication in Business*,[28] *Communication for Management and Business*,[29] and *Reporting Technical Information*.[30] If you now own a textbook, you'll find it handy as a reference. If you don't, you can do without it.

[23]New York: W. W. Norton, 1954.

[24]Calvin F. and Stanton E. Schmid, 2nd ed. (New York: John Wiley, 1979).

[25]New York: McGraw-Hill, 1969.

[26]New York: Van Nostrand Reinhold, 1981.

[27]San Jose, Calif.: Sorcim Corp., 1983.

[28]Donald J. Leonard, 4th ed. (New York: McGraw-Hill, 1979).

[29]Norman B. Sigband, 2nd ed. (Glenview, Ill.: Scott Foresman, 1976).

[30]Kenneth W. Houp and Thomas E. Pearsall, 2nd ed. (New York: Glencoe Press, 1973).

Index

May we introduce other Ten Speed Books you will find useful...
over three million people have

What Color Is Your Parachute?
by Richard N. Bolles

Based upon the latest research this annually revised and updated manual is designed to give the most practical step-by-step help imaginable to the job-hunter or career-changer, whether he or she is sixteen or sixty-five. Questions asked throughout the cross-country research upon which the book is based, were: What methods of job-hunting and career-changing work best? What new methods have been developed by the best minds in the field? Is it possible to change jobs without going back for lengthy retraining?

6 × 9 inches, 384 pages, $8.95 paper, $15.95 cloth

Finding Facts Fast
How to Find Out What You Want And Need to Know
by Alden Todd

"...may well be the best of how-to-do-research books on the market today."

—*Writers' Digest*

"...covers most imaginable ways to get information quickly."

—*Village Voice*

6 × 9 inches, 160 pages, illustrated, $3.95 paper

Better Letters
by Jan Venolia

Better Letters is an up-to-date handbook designed to improve writing style and to make letters pleasing to the eye. The book includes sample letters that can be used as guides; advice on personal as well as business correspondence; a concise bibliography; an index; and an appendix with a variety of aids for the writer. Also included is a section not found in other books on avoiding sexist terms.

6 × 9 inches, 160 pages, $5.95 paper, $7.95 spiral, $9.95 cloth

Write Right!
by Jan Venolia

Write Right! is a handy format desk-drawer digest whose aim is simply to be a combination first-aid kit and preventive maintenance manual for the written word. Concentrating on everyday nagging problems, *Write Right!* effectively simplifies the fine points of English grammar, punctuation, spelling and style.

5⅜ × 7 inches, 128 pages, $4.95 paper, $5.95 spiral

Louder & Funnier
A Practical Guide For Overcoming Stagefright in Speechmaking
by Bob Nelson

"Here are methods to overcome excessive stage fright, including a "fear map" to help chart your way to calmer nerves, relaxation techniques, ways to build memory and be better prepared, and how to involve your audience in your presentation."
—Changing Times

"He deals with why stage fright is normal, the benefits of fear, why we fear, and how to construct a model for overcoming stage fright..."
—St. Paul Pioneer Press/Dispatch

6 × 9 inches, 196 pages, $5.95 paper

Mail Order Moonlighting
by Cecil C. Hoge, Sr.

"This is the authoritative and best up-to-date word for anyone in the mail order business or planning to start one. No baloney, the real thing in a field full of phony books. Every useful detail is covered.

"Cecil Hoge, Sr. deserves the title 'Sr.'"
—The Next Whole Earth Catalog

6 × 9 inches, 416 pages, $8.95 paper

You'll find them in your bookstore or library, or you can order directly from us. Please include $1.00 additional for each book's shipping and handling.

TEN SPEED PRESS
P.O. Box 7123   Berkeley, California 94707

MA